Sundays At The Fields

Thoughts and meditations for busy softball families

Heather Davis

Cover Design by Lisa Kuehn of Dream On Marketing
Interior Design by Road Trip Media, LLC
Published by Road Trip Media, LLC

ISBN-13: 978-1530011155
ISBN-10: 1530011159

Also available in eBook publication.
Printed in the United States of America.

For the softball coaches who take young girls and mold amazing athletes and adults ...

Specifically Heather Hawthorne, Adam Shelley, Erica Derryberry, Melissa Furnas, Ryan Davis, Cat Nitz, Cody Barham, and Catherine Reeves ...

Especially our Oklahoma Rebelz coaches, Ryan Higbee and Mike Barnes ...

And especially, *especially* Brian Davis, or as Briley knows him, Daddy.

Introduction

When I was a senior in high school, two things happened. The first was that Guideposts did not award me their high school writing scholarship and the second was that the United Methodist Church did not award me the Bishop's scholarship. These things meant that I would not be a published author before I graduated high school, nor would I become an ordained clergy person.

At the time, I was pretty mad at both entities because they were obviously making a big mistake. Or so I thought. Now, I realize that those *No*s were because God had bigger *Yes*es in mind. (I learned that from my girls who learned it from church during a study on dating. Thanking Jesus right now that other folks are talking to them about this as well!)

I am now a published author, a middle school teacher, a wife and a momma. My life is pretty amazing. With our being a full-fledged, up-to-our-earlobes softball family, I felt a nudging to go back to my roots ... ya know, my high school roots. I wanted to write about faith in the context of softball. So many of our Sundays were spent at the softball fields. We have a great softball family, Oklahoma Rebelz, and on the Sundays that we play, one of the parents always makes sure to give the girls some devotion time. God truly does meet us where we are—

even at the softball fields. But I know there are some softball families that don't get their Sunday morning devotion time. I'm hoping this book helps them to see God with them at the fields.

There are fifty-two entries within this book—just like fifty-two Sundays in a year. I hope you don't spend every single Sunday at the softball field (but that would be kinda awesome). I do hope that when you find yourself playing ball that you'll remember to pull out this book and find some time with your Maker.

I am not a Bible Scholar. I am not a Pastor. I am a momma who loves her God, loves her family and loves the game of softball.

Play Ball!

Practice Makes ...

Don't be conformed to the patterns of this world, but
be transformed by the renewing of your minds so that you
can figure out what God's will is—
what is good, pleasing and mature.
Romans 12:2

Mornings do not go well at our house. They usually start with all the members of our family hitting snooze multiple times on our respective alarm devices. Then we follow that up with frantic rushing and general chaos. When it's time for us to all leave the house, we end our mornings shouting.

Don't forget your lunch!

Did you write your monarch butterfly report?

Where's your practice bag?

Is your geometry test today?

Don't forget to stay after school to get your essay back.

Finally, we are off—my husband, Brian, taking our older daughter, Hadley to high school while our younger kid, Briley, heads to middle school with me. I'm willing to bet that at least three out of five days, one of us returns to the house because we've forgotten something or another. One time, we had to turn around because one of us (she shall remain nameless) forgot her shoes. Her shoes!

The funny thing is that every morning, at least during the school year, the routine should be the same: Get up, get ready, load up and go. Why, then, is it so frantic?

It's simple: We are not prepared for the morning the night before. We have not practiced.

Practice.

It seems silly to practice our mornings. What would that look like? Would we all lie in bed at 4:30 in the afternoon until my husband blows a whistle and then we each move through our morning routines. If Briley accidently brushed her teeth when Hadley should've been at the sink, would Brian blow the whistle again so we would have to start the "practice morning" over? It seems a little bit ridiculous—and quite frankly, we wouldn't have the time to do it.

But, when we talk about practicing plays on the field or practicing situations with our team, it's not ridiculous at all. In fact, practice is what makes the difference between going home with the trophy and just going home.

When I coached my daughter's t-ball team, we practiced hitting and fielding and running. We even practiced proper stances. We were learning the game and if our players wanted to continue on with softball, they needed to know the basics.

Now that we've been playing softball for almost ten years, the one thing that does change is practice. Every aspect of softball is practiced so that in a game situation, the players know what to do.

Can you imagine if you rounded second and then stopped dead and yelled, "Time out! I can't remember where I run to next." Or if you snagged a grounder at short stop then said, "What should I do with this ball now?"

I'm willing to bet that you'd not only be thrown out, but you might be taken out of the game. You might also get to see your coach have an actual heart attack.

And while our coach is willing to advise you during the game, he (or she) ultimately wants you to be able to play the game at an expert level, without distractions confusing you.

Paul's letter to the Romans calls for us to practice living a Godly life at all times. We are cautioned against doing what the world wants us to do—sleep in, be lazy, rush around, allow chaos to rule our lives. Instead we should renew our minds: This means practice. Paul's letter tells us that practicing how God wants us to live will allow us to see his will—his game plan, if you will—clearly.

And as a result of this practice, we will surely go home with the trophy.

Heavenly Father, we know that You call us to practice living a life that is pleasing to You every day. We don't know all the situations that life will bring to us, but we know that You want us to live in such a way that others know we are Your children. Renew us when we tire of practice and strengthen us when it seems too hard for us to continue. In Jesus' name we pray, Amen.

-2-

The Pile of Laundry Is High

*Lord, you have been our help, generation after
generation. Before the mountains were born, before you
birthed the earth and the inhabited world—from forever
in the past to forever in the future, you are God.*
Psalm 90:1-2

One of my favorite tournaments to travel to is the World Series in Shawnee, Oklahoma. It's near a big city, and it's extended over several days so it's not non-stop games. We get to chill with our team, eat sit-down meals, hang out in the big city at night … it's just a great week.

Now, understand that once the pool play is over and bracket play begins, it's serious softball time. But until then, it's just a nice time to play a little softball and enjoy our team family.

Then, after five days at the tourney, win or lose, we return home. And we unpack. I haven't been to every team member's home the day after the World Series, but I'm assuming it's not much different than our home.

We have our softball hangover—we wake up late, watch junk television, check in on social media and see how many likes our Instagram picture of a winning run received.

Then we unpack.

As the main laundry-doer in our family, I usually ask everyone to bring their dirty laundry to the laundry room.

And for the next few days, I chip away at the dirty laundry mountain. The use of the word *mountain* is not a hyperbole. The dirty laundry following this particular tournament can sometimes pile as high as washer and dryer. I could literally jump into the mountain of dirty laundry and not be seen.

(Please note that I wouldn't do this because the tournament is at the end of July and that means it is filthy with our sweat stink!)

It takes forever for the laundry mountain to be dwindled into neatly folded piles of clean laundry.

Actually, forever is an hyperbole—it really only takes days.

And, it's actually not a mountain—it's really just a lot of dirty, smelly clothing.

So, the truth of the matter is this: It takes me days to get through a big pile of dirty laundry.

You know what it took God days to do? CREATE THE WHOLE WORLD!

Let's think about this for a minute:

It took six runs and five innings to win our way into the final bracket.

It took thirty-three pitches to win a tournament.

It took over fifty at-bats for my daughter to hit her first homerun.

It took a five-day tournament to make about ten loads of laundry.

And ...

It took God six days to create the world.

13

To craft the mountains.

To fill the seas.

To set the wind in motion.

To pitch the moon into the sky and to plant the sun as the center of our universe.

To birth human kind in His own image.

Seven days, y'all.

It's a pretty amazing God we serve who created this world for us. But, let's take it a little bit further.

Before the creation, there is God. Before we were born, there is God. Before each tournament we play, there is God.

After the laundry is done, there is God. After the trophies have been placed high in our rooms, there is God. After we've finished our softball careers, there is God.

After our memories of the game we love have faded and the mountains of laundry cease to exist, there is God.

When the laundry pile is high, our God is higher. When the trophy is big, our God is bigger.

When we win, when we lose, when we drive away from the softball fields at the end of the weekend, our God is there.

He's a pretty big and pretty amazing God. Bigger and more amazing than even the biggest pile of laundry.

God of all creation, who goes before us and follows behind us, help us to never lose sight of how big and how great You are. Remind us daily of Your might and Your greatness and help us to give thanks that while we may have high mountains of dirty laundry, we also have mountains of beauty made for us by our Creator. Amen and amen.

-3-

Listen To Me

My sheep listen to my voice. I know them, and they
follow me.
John 10:27

I watch as my daughter spanks the big yellow ball to the hole in left field. My eyes scan the field to watch the ball drop untouched, and then I begin cheering. The rest of our team parents join right in. The two players that were on first and second begin racing around the bags, heading toward home. Our cheers get louder and louder.

The other teams' fans begin cheering as well, but with shouts of "Throw to second!" "Get her at home!" "Gun the ball in!"

Then, for what appears to be no reason at all. Our runner stops at third, my kiddo slides into second, and the third runner slides into home just before the ball finds its way to the catcher.

The catcher does her job and lays a tag on our runner, but the official has already called her safe.

I had no idea the ball had flown threw the air toward home.

"Wow!" I exclaim to my husband. "They acted quick!"

"Who did?" he asks as he enters the plays into his scorekeeping app.

"The fielders! The runners! I was so caught up in the great hit that I had no idea the ball was that close to getting her out."

He rolled his eyes at me, as he often does at the fields. Then I hear the third base coach hollers, "Nice hit, Briley!"

That's my kid. The hitter, not the coach. She gives a nod, brushes off her pants from the slide and gets ready to run again.

The next player hits the ball into the same left-field hole, and the cheering starts again.

The runners are flying around the bases and the fielders are shouting commands and preparing to receive the ball. Then, just like that, the play is stopped. The hitter is on third and our other two runners have scored.

This time, I noticed something: The coaches? They were not standing idly by in the dug outs or waiting for the runner on third base as if waiting for a bus. They, too were shouting out instructions—typically one word.

The defensive coaches were shouting out the base the players should throw to.

Home!

Third!

The offensive coaches were commanding.

Stay!

Go! Go!

Up!

All the players really had to do was keep focused on their one job and listen for the one voice that counts: Their coach's voice.

God calls us to do just one job at a time. We are, often times, too burdened by the weight of the world—our friends, our work, our home life—that His one calling gets lost and shoved to the side. The good news is this: God can see it all and He's calling our plays.

If Briley had listened to me and run past second, which is what I hollered for her to do, she and possibly the other runner would have been called out.

On the field, she has to tune out voices from the stands and the dugouts and the other fields. She has to tune out the birds and the insects and even the other players at times. She has to focus in on the voice of the coach.

When I yelled, "Run!" he yelled, "Hold!"

I was focused on my kid scoring. He was focused on the game as a whole.

God is an all-knowing God. He sees not only the one solitary runner, but He sees every single runner in every single game. He knows what we should be doing, when we should be doing it and where.

Throughout it all, He calls to us.

Go!

Hold!

Feed!

Love!

His voice can be heard loud and clear above the rest of the noise that the world makes. We just have to listen for it.

Holy God, whose voice is like nothing else in this world, speak to us, cause us to stop and listen, direct our paths and keep us on the task You've created us for. Teach us to tune out the world and direct our minds, our thoughts and our ears to You and You alone. In the name of our Lord, Jesus Christ, Amen.

-4-

The Off-season

Through laziness, the roof sags;
through idle hands, the house leaks.
Ecclesiastes 10:18

A lot had happened during the previous year. We had changed softball teams, gotten a new car, sold an old truck, traveled more than 50,000 miles, and started a new business. I published two books, and my mom had a stroke, went through rehab and moved in with us.

So, when we found ourselves with exactly six weeks between the fall season and the spring season (I guess those six weeks would be called *winter!*), we did nothing. We let our pitcher decide if she wanted her pitching lessons each week. She chose to take a lesson every so often. But for the most part, we all allowed ourselves some much-needed downtime.

We enjoyed our break, but we were also ready to get back into the swing of softball. So, when the team announced their first schedule of practices and tournaments, my softballer, Briley, was giddy at the prospect of being with her teammates, her coaches and playing with the big yellow ball that she loves so much.

The first practice, though, returned home a frustrated pitcher.

Her drop ball no longer dropped, her change up didn't change, and her fast ball had lost a few miles per hour.

"But I practiced!" she lamented as she tossed her glove to the side, plopping herself on the couch.

Her daddy gently reminded her that while she did practice, it was not with the same regularity or intensity that she had done during the season.

"Can I still be as good as I was last year?" she moaned with her cold-sleeved arm over her face.

We both assured her that she could.

"But," Brian interjected, "You'll have to put in the work. We'll have to pick up the pace of our lessons and extra practices."

She nodded. She was willing to do whatever it took to get her wicked change-up back in her arsenal.

This is very much the way we are with any aspect of our lives.

We exercise, lose a few pounds and then stop, thinking the momentum will continue.

We clean the house and expect it to stay clean.

We wash one load of laundry and seem perplexed when there are two more loads ready to go by the time the weekend rolls around.

We make a new friend and then wonder why we don't get together more often.

We feel close to God and in touch with His word and then feel lost when we close our Bibles and forget to hem our days in prayer.

It takes very little for us to fall out of practice, out of shape, out of touch, out of step ... out of hope.

The good news is that it also takes very little for us to fall right back into those things ... depending how hard we are to work on them.

God leads us down paths he wants us to follow, but He doesn't necessarily make the pathway clear; that's on us. That's part of our journey.

If pitchers could throw strikes without any effort, we'd probably all still be playing t-ball.

If batters hit home runs every single time, the game would be boring.

If believers had a perfect faith, there'd be no reason for us to take time with God, to depend upon Him, to seek His face in everything that we do and there'd be no reason for us to share His love.

We must work continually on the goals we have set for ourselves, and in all things, seek God and His grace.

Simply put, we cannot be lazy in any aspect of our lives.

Heavenly Father of all good things, allow us rest when we are weary, but strength when we need to carry on. Make Your will the focus of our goals and lift us up when we become lazy. In Your most holy name we pray, Amen.

-5-

Looking Good

Even the hairs on your head are all counted. Don't be afraid. You are worth more than many sparrows.
Matthew 10:30-31

The night before Briley's first big tournament with a competitive team, we spent, what seemed like hours, pouring over potential hairstyles for my kid.

We needed something that would be durable—it would have to withstand the facemask and batting helmet being put on and removed at least a dozen times.

We needed something that would be cute. One of the teammates had made them all matching ribbons, so we'd want to show that off.

Finally, we needed something that would be practical—she wouldn't be able to have a successful tournament day if she were constantly having to move her hair away from her face.

We settled on a really cute bang-braid off to the side that led into a French braid and then a pony tail. I snapped her picture, Instagrammed it and away we went.

The first game was kinda rough, as it is the first time you do anything different. The facemask and the

23

helmet took their toll on the Pinterest-worthy 'do. Before the third game even started, her hair was in a ponytail and wisps were teasing her eyes and tickling her ears. We had a break before the fourth game, during which we ran to the store and purchased some head bands.

This whole hair-in-the-face fiasco didn't stop us from trying to create some cute hair for other tournaments. Eventually, we were able to master some nice 'dos that actually stayed in place without our shaving the strays or trimming the spare hairs.

But honestly, at the end of a tournament day, when the helmet and facemask are both tucked away in her bag and we're heading back to the car leaving behind great memories and a significant trail of field dirt, I couldn't tell you what her hair was supposed to look like. It's matted with sweat and dust and chalk and even a few sunflower seed hulls. It's not even remotely close to how we intended it to look when we started out eight, ten, twelve, or even sixteen hours before.

After a long, hot shower and a good dose of shampoo and conditioner, Briley looks like her old self again. Her straight, brown, mid-back length hair is combed and doesn't look like woodland animals have frolicked in it. And it's beautiful ... just like she is.

God created us all beautiful. He knows every line on our palms, He designed every wrinkle on our toes, and He's counted every hair on our heads. He knows our steps before we make them. He knows our thoughts before we think them.

He knows which balls we'll swing at and which strikes will sail right before our eyes and into the catcher's mitt. And He knows which stray hairs will fall from our perfectly-plaited braid before we even step foot on the field.

He knows our losses and our wins before they're recorded in the scorebook. He knows our triumphs before we take home the trophies, and He knows the heartaches before we hang our heads on the way to the car at the end of a long, dirty, hot day ... with the sweat, hair and tears mingling on our faces.

And, He loves us so much that He's willing to sift through the matted, ratted hair on our heads and count the strands.

He made us beautiful. He made us strong. And, He's proud of us as His creations.

Heavenly creator, who knows every little bitty part of our bodies, our minds and our spirits: Help us to remember that You have made us and You have called us to reflect Your love to a sometimes dirty world. Even though our hair may be messy and our face may be streaked with sweat, tears and sometimes blood, You love us when we are clean and when we are dirty. Thank You for that love and thank You for knowing us better than we can even know ourselves. In Your all-knowing name we pray, Amen.

-6-

Dear Second Place Team

Now I urge you to be encouraged. Not one of your
lives will be lost,
though we lose the ship.
Acts 27: 22

Dear Second Place Team ... and all the teams who go home without a trophy,

Thanks for a great game.

You may not feel like it right now, but you played a great game. In one aspect or another, the winning team learned something from you. Maybe they learned that they can turn a double play on the very first bat. Maybe they learned that your short stop has a wicked arm and can gun a ball even when laying flat on her belly. Maybe they learned that your new chant when we change pitchers is catchy—and quite a useful distraction.

It was a great game indeed.

And while you are not going home with that trophy, hold your head up high. Whether you finished very last or second place overall or anywhere in between, you showed up on the fields today. You came with your best equipment, the talents you've been given and a team that's willing to get dirty with you. You sunk your cleats into the field and had nothing on your mind but winning.

26

The good news is this: There will be another game. There will be another tournament. There will be another season. Your game is not going away. In the history of all sports, there have been very few games that have become completely extinct, and I promise you this much: This game that you love is here to stay.

And the next time you play, you'll be a better team than you were when the victor's scored their winning run.

It stings—trust me, I know. But, you are not alone in your defeat. Your coaches, your family, your fans … they all share in your heartbreak. But don't let it keep you down.

God offers many promises to those who go home without a trophy. In Jeremiah, we are promised peaceful plans full of a future hope. We read about a champion's wreath that is waiting for us in 2 Timothy. In Acts 22, we are assured that we will not lose our lives even though the ship sinks.

Funny thing about that word *ship*: Many final games in tournaments are referred to as the ship—short for championship.

Does this mean God is a sports fan? Maybe, but more than that, He's *your* fan. The talents that you bring with you, either to the field, the classroom, the playground, in your home, at your church … those talents came directly from our Heavenly Father. He knew that you'd have a passion for this game and that you would need the strong arm or the fast legs or the keen eye.

He gave you the talents you need to succeed.

27

Did you win this game? Nope. Will you even win another game? Who knows? But, you played well, using the skills and talents God gave to you and only you.

Chin up.

And thanks for a great game.

Heavenly Father who gives us good gifts, help us to remember that even when we fall short of the trophy, there's so much more to life than winning. You have given us talents to use to glorify You—whether we win or not. And that's more important than any gold trophy or medal or ring, we'll take home at the end of a 'ship. In Jesus' good name we pray, Amen.

-7-

Thunderbolts and Lightning—
Very, Very Frightening

Because He will order His messengers to help you,
To protect you wherever you go.
Psalms 91:11

We watched the storm clouds form just to the south and west of the complex. If we stayed in the winner's bracket, we were bound to be here for at least four more hours. As the current game was winding down, the clouds became darker. I looked around the stands. There was not one parent who didn't have his or her smart phone out checking the radar.

The complex was on the outskirts of an area that had been hit by tornados on at least three different occasions in the past twenty-five years. That thought, I'm sure, was lingering in each mom and dad's mind.

"They'll have to delay while this storms blows through," one parent finally spoke. We all murmured our agreement. The winning run slid home and the game was over. We were scheduled to play again in fifteen minutes.

Then we saw the first lightning strike.

29

Lightning is dangerous in any locale, but to be in a place filled with metal bleachers, metal bats and chain link fences, it was a very scary situation.

Our coaches pulled the girls off the field, and sent us to our cars until the storm passed.

Then the umps did something that was worse than the lightning. They called for the game to start.

"We haven't seen any more lightning," they said as we gathered the players and waited for the coach to make a decision.

"You'll either play or forfeit," the umps demanded, having to practically shout over the thunder.

This was the state tournament. We'd played the whole season to get here. We were ranked in the top ten, nationwide. This tournament should be ours.

The coach looked at the faces of the girls who wanted to play just as much as they wanted to take shelter. We saw in his face the disappointment and devastation that he was about to pass to our players in his decision to forfeit. He just couldn't quite verbalize it yet.

The rain began to fall as if God himself had turned the faucet on full blast. We could barely see in front of our own eyes. While we couldn't see the lightning, we heard thunder—claps louder than any softball mom cheering. It was dangerous.

"We are not going out there," a parent spoke up. "You will delay the game. We're not putting any of these kids in danger."

Then another parent spoke, "It won't be a forfeit. It will be a delay."

And another spoke, "I'll go get the tournament director."

In the end, we ended up waiting out the storm in our cars. The storm blew in and stayed for a while. We didn't resume our play for over an hour. Had we chosen to play, I can't imagine the danger we'd have put precious lives in—the lives of our players and their teammates.

There are times when people pull us into dangerous situations, either through threats, manipulation or other falsehearted means. When passions run high and emotions are on the surface, it's easy to get caught up and meet them at the unsafe juncture. Jesus came to show us that we can always be connected to our Heavenly Father. He truly does send protectors for us at every turn.

Jesus, our keeper, thank You for not only showing us how to have a loving, safe relationship with God, our father, but showing us that God sends protectors to walk with us, to stand up with us, to help us when the storms rage. Thank You for being the first protector and showing us the way. In Your name we pray. Amen.

-8-

A Wagon Full

From His fullness, we have all received
grace upon grace.
John 1:16

"You'll need a wagon," a veteran softball mom advised us before we went to our first competitive tournament with our then-nine-year-old daughter.

I later shook my head and scoffed. "We won't need a wagon."

After all, she was nine. It was a round-robin, one-day tournament. They'd play three games and we'd go home. Easy enough. A wagon would just be a cumbersome burden.

I braided Briley's hair as my hubby loaded the vehicle. Then we drove an hour to the complex, dropping our little baller off at the gate so she could catch up with her team and begin warming up.

We parked about three-football fields away from the fields, give or take two-hundred and fifty yards. While my older daughter and I stood at the back of the vehicle, my husband began unloading.

We had two small ice chests: One with sports drinks and waters, and one with snacks. He unloaded several blankets, including a big denim, puffy blanket for our girl to sleep on when she got tired. He unloaded our lawn chairs, in case the seating was taken or we wanted a different view. He unloaded a duffle bag full of sunscreen, bug spray, lip balm, Icy-Hot, sunglasses, toothbrushes, toothpaste, washrags, towels and wet wipes.

The three of us, like pack mules, grabbed what we could and dragged ourselves into the complex.

We looked like complete and total amateurs. Parents who had been in the competitive circuit longer than we had walked by us pulling their wagons, their backs light and free. Some of them smirked, and I could almost hear their thoughts of *newbies* and *bless their hearts.* Some of them ignored us, not acknowledging the problem of the wagonless, hoping we would go away.

Before we were even inside the gate, my older daughter had questioned her choice to support her sister, deeming a day at home by herself doing laundry would be better than dragging all of our "essentials" to the fields.

Before the next tournament, we had a wagon.

The things we carried were all things that were essential and necessary, let's be clear about that. But they were also things that we had from our abundance. Not every gifted athlete is afforded the opportunity to play her sport because not every family has the means to involve themselves in the demanding schedule (and budget) that athletics sometimes requires.

It struck me as ironic that we were carrying our blessings with a grumbling spirit.

Unfortunately, we do this all too often.

Jesus came as a sacrifice to give us endless blessings and to pour grace into our lives and onto us as though they were a sprinkler on a lush, green outfield. Many times, we take these gifts with complaint and without gratitude. Instead, we should prepare ourselves to accept what God lavishes upon us and enter the playing field with a full wagon.

We all need wagons—the newbies and the novices. We need to figuratively believe that wherever we go, the gifts of our Father's unfailing love will be so great that we need wagons to carry everything He gives to us.

Giving and generous God, we know that You love to shower us with blessings, grace, gifts and goodness. Forgive us when we complain and fail to acknowledge the gifts. Allow us to be gracious when we receive these things from You and to pull our grace-filled wagons with a light and grateful heart. In the name of Your sacrificial Son we offer our thanks, Amen.

-9-

Face Off

As iron sharpens iron, so friends sharpen each other.
-Proverbs 27:17

The first competitive team that our daughter played for faced some challenges and, unfortunately, the team didn't survive. Most of the girls quickly found other teams, as did our daughter, but they had already played several tournaments together. Their friendships had been solidified. And then torn apart.

Our new team was a great fit. We quickly saw how this could be a positive move in her softball career, as much as a nine-year-old can have a career. She was happy, we were happy, softball was happening.

Then, there came a tournament when our little pitcher had to face off against one of her former teammates.

"Oh no! We're playing against her!" Briley lamented. "She's a good hitter!"

"And you," her daddy reassured her, "are a good pitcher."

"But what if I strike her out?" she nervously continued.

"Then you strike her out," her daddy retorted.

35

Then our daughter caught her breath. "What if she hits a home run?"

"Then she hits a home run. Just get out there and do what you know to do."

Eventually, her former teammate approached the plate and our little pitcher lobbed a couple of leisurely pitches right down the gut. The batter fouled them both off.

After the second foul, the batter stepped from the box and took a few practice swings, looking at nothing in particular. Our pitcher filled some divots with her foot facing away from the plate.

Briley turned back to face her former teammate, and the batter stepped into the box. The catcher gave the sign, and Briley nodded her head slightly acknowledging the pitch. The intensity on the face of both batter and hitter was tangible. The wind-up started and the pitcher cocked her bat. The yellow ball flew down the gut and the batter swung her bat down the line as if she were swinging for the stands ...

At the end of the game, each team lined up and "good gamed" each other. When Briley got to her former teammate, they bumped fists, then they grinned widely, stretching it into a laugh and finally falling into each other's arms in a bear hug.

They had survived the face off and lived to tell the tale.

I can't recall us facing this particular player again—we've seen her at tournaments, but our teams haven't met in bracket play. The girls still smile and greet each other with hugs.

I'm sure you're wondering what happened—did Briley strike her out? Did the hitter get a piece of the ball yet again?

I truly cannot remember.

More importantly, it really doesn't matter.

What does matter is that these girls—these friends—learned a valuable lesson that day. When they are facing a friend who is opposed to them, they do what they are called to do, but at the end of the day, they still love each other.

We face people on a daily basis with whom we are opposed—maybe it's politics, maybe it's our child-rearing philosophies, maybe it's just that we don't get along. This doesn't mean that we stop being who we were made to be when we're around these people. This means that we continue to follow our call in life with respect and dignity.

When we stay true to the person we were created to be, we can only make the world a better place ... we can only make the people we encounter better.

God of all people, we ask for strength to be ourselves in adverse situations. We ask for respectful people to cross our paths, and we ask that in all of our ways and in all of our actions, we bring glory to You, our wonderful and strong creator. Amen.

-10-

Just A Little Bump

I'm convinced that nothing can separate us from God's love in Christ Jesus our Lord: Not death or life, not angels or rules, not present things or future things, not powers or height or depth or any other thing that is created.
Romans 8: 38-39

It was the last week of school—the last week of elementary school!—and my daughter was complaining of a headache.

"If you stay home from school, you'll miss your last elementary field trip," I "threatened" one morning, hoping to stop her complaining.

She sighed and agreed to go to school.

That evening, she was still complaining of a headache.

"If you still have a headache tomorrow, I'm going to take you to the doctor." I just knew she was overwhelmed with her field trip and the last day of school and was just complaining to be complaining.

She sighed and said, "Okay." Then she leaned into me for a hug and whimpered.

This was serious. We love our doctor, but we don't necessarily like going to our doctor.

The next day, after a series of physical and mental tests administered by our doctor and on the computer, it was determined that Briley had a concussion.

What's more is that she didn't even receive it on the softball field. Wednesday night, she'd participated in our church's talent show, singing an Amy Grant song (which is what you sing when your momma grew up in the 80s and 90s). As she went with the group of kids who participated in the finale up to the stage, a metal divider fell and bonked her on the head. But, she's tough. She's been hit by softballs traveling at high rates of speed. She's been banged on the helmet with a bat at almost-full speed. She'd slid into a base and collided with two other players. How was it that doing something so benign as singing could result in a concussion?

The worst news was that she was out of softball for two weeks. No hitting lessons, no pitching lessons, no team practice, no playing catch in the front yard with her dad. The most activity the doctor would allow was moving from the couch to the bathroom when nature called.

For a kid who's addicted to the sport she loves, this was a long and hard two weeks. When we returned to our favorite doctor's office for a reevaluation, we were nervous. My kiddo was afraid she'd never play ball again. My husband was afraid that she'd be set back so much that she'd have to start over at square one. I was afraid my child wouldn't progress back to health like she should.

After a full-regime of evaluations, she was deemed healthy and was given the okay to slowly ease back into softball. We all sighed a collective sigh of relief.

For those two weeks, though, there was some soul-searching happening in our house—even Briley's older sister, Hadley, who doesn't play softball was concerned. "What will we do all summer if she can't play ball?" she asked at dinner one night.

Fortunately for us, we acclimated easily right back into our softball life.

Thankfully for us as well, we have a conviction from Paul that there's nothing on this earth—nothing at all—that can separate us from God's love through Jesus. Even in death, Paul says, he's convinced we'll be connected to our Heavenly Father's love.

Concussions are scary, let's be clear about that. Thinking about having to give up a favorite sport or activity or even a friendship hurts our hearts. But, Christ came as a bridge to keep us at all times connected to the love of God ... and that's not scary at all. That's a promise that can see us through any situation we find ourselves in. Even when we have concussions from talent shows.

God of healing who loves us so much, thank You for Christ Jesus who connects us to You at all times. Thank You that there's nothing on this earth that can keep us from You for any reason. In Your love-filled name we pray. Amen.

-11-

Yum! Yum!

Eating too much honey isn't good, nor is it
appropriate to seek honor.
A person without self-control is like a breached city,
one with no walls.
Proverbs 25: 27-28

There's a complex that we play in once a season, and it's my favorite tournament of the year for one reason: French fries.

Now, I'm not a big French fry fan, per se. I mean, I'll eat them because I don't want to get hungry later on in the day. And, of course, if there's brown gravy or a chocolate shake involved, I do like dipping my fries in some brown gravy and a chocolate shake. (But not gravy and shakes together ... ew.)

If we're standing in line at a softball complex food court, I'm not going to order just fries. Unless, of course, we're at Firelake in Shawnee, OK.

These fries, my friends are lightly battered and then fried to a delectable crispiness and then sprinkled with some amazing seasoning salt. They are served in a gigantic serving boat. Wait ... not serving boat. Serving cruise liner. And? They are beyond delicious.

41

Now, I've given this some great thought. The very first time I ate these fries, I was starving. I'd had half of a sandwich and a few pieces of watermelon for the entire day. It was approximately three hundred degrees Celsius, and I'd drunk two gallons of water and sweated four gallons of salty sweat. I might have been a little bit in need of sustenance of any kind when my older daughter bought the world's most amazing fries and sat down beside me in the stands.

"Can I have one?" I begged, with a slight sob. After receiving the affirmative answer to my question, I gobbled down about a pound of the starchy manna from heaven.

Then I bought myself my own order of fries. That is not a lie, friends! I ate two orders of fries on a very hot day while sitting in the bright sun. It shouldn't have ended pretty, but it did. I did not get sick. I didn't even get the slightest of stomach aches. So, you now what I did the next day?

I ordered more fries.

The next year when we returned to Firelake, I couldn't wait to get more fries. In fact, my player might have asked me if I thought she could hit one to the fences during this year and I might have said, "I don't know, but I can't wait to get more fries."

We ate out of the complex a couple of times; once at a local BBQ joint that had been featured at *Diners, Drive-thrus and Dives*, and once at a hamburger joint that has been around for over fifty years. I refused to order fries there because we were at Firelake and I knew they had good fries.

And, true to my word, I ate fries like they provided the eater with an endless fount of youth.

At the end of the weekend, however, I felt like I was sweating peanut oil. And by the time we were driving home, I was kinda, sorta praying for a stomach bug that would somehow cause me to throw up everything I'd eaten for the past four days.

Proverbs would refer to me as a breached city with no walls. Others might refer to me as a beached whale. Both descriptions are fitting.

We were not created to be overindulgent beings. In fact, the very first warning God gives to us is about overindulge with a certain apple in a certain garden. And even though honey is sweet (and Firelake's French fries are delish), too much is not good.

Proverbs tells us that self-control can keep us from looking like a beached whale ... and a breached city. Ya know, whatever metaphor fits.

You are in control, God. We are weak and cannot always be left to make our own decisions. We come to You for strength. We come to You for control. We come to You seeking your guidance in helping us to walk the path of honor, health and happiness. In Jesus' name we pray, Amen.

-12-
The Christ-like Star

*Then Jesus went into the temple and threw out all
those who were selling and buying there. He pushed over
the tables used for currency exchange and the chairs of
those who sold doves. He said to them, "It's written My
house will be called a house of prayer. But you've made it
a hideout for crooks."*
Matthew 21: 12-13

During the off-season (also known as winter), our
girls played basketball. In our town, for their age, the
basketball options were very limited. So, we played in a
league that gave each player a star at the end of each
game that was supposed to accentuate her strengths
during the game.

Our daughter didn't get along with one particular
player from another team. They didn't necessarily talk
trash (they were only eight years old at the time), but
they didn't like to meet up with each other on the court.
Usually, the coaches and the referees had to separate
them when our team met with theirs.

Toward the end of the season, we met this team yet
again. And yet again, Briley and this other player were
all over each other ... but the official was doing nothing

to shut it down. The coaches, maybe they were tired from a long season, were doing nothing to get their behaviors under control.

We'd talked to Briley about turning the other cheek and doing the right thing regardless of what everyone else is doing and being a leader and not a follower. But, we also didn't want her to be run over. When it was clear that no adult was going to put an end to the girls' aggressions and it was clear that Briley was about to explode, my husband tried to talk to the official during a time out, letting him know that this had been a feud that had been fueled all season long and someone would get hurt. The official essentially said, "Kids will be kids."

When play resumed, the fight was on. Literally. Briley took an elbow to her gut as she was going up for a shot, and the other kid ended up on her back on the hardwood. At that point, the adults got involved. The girls sat out and didn't get to share the floor with each other anymore during that game.

Afterwards, when the coaches were handing out the stars, they unhesitatingly gave Briley the Christ-like star. With a confused little face, she turned to me and said, "What's this star mean?"

Typically, the Christ-like star was given to the player who'd shown the best sportsmanship. But, today, I'm assuming, the Christ-like star was given to the kid who behaved most like Jesus ... in the temple ... with the crooks and the scoundrels.

Sometimes there's a point when all of us turn over tables and throw people out of our lives because they are not honoring our homes. The story of Jesus in the temple shows us a very human side to Christ, a side that

45

we can learn from, a side that we can sometimes emulate if the situation is exactly right and the passions are high and the welfare of our brothers or sisters is at stake.

Most of the time, though—especially on the basketball courts or the ball fields or at dance classes or even in, *especially in*, the lines at Hellmart—we are called to not be like Jesus in the temple, but like Jesus outside of the temple: healing, ministering, listening, hugging, feeding, clothing.

Jesus who was just like us, hold us close and guide our words, our actions and our thoughts to be like Yours. Help us to know the time to turn over a table and the time to turn the other cheek. And in all things that we do, help us to do them with the same love and grace that You give to us. In Your compassionate and passionate name we pray, Amen.

-13-
Worn Out Cleats

*Youths will become tired and weary, young men will
certainly stumble; but those who hope in the Lord will
renew their strength; they will fly up on wings like eagles;
they will run and not be tired;
they will walk and not be weary.*
Isaiah 40:30-31

For whatever reason, Brian was home and I found myself in the big city at the sporting goods store with Briley, who had convinced me that she needed new cleats. This was the first mistake.

"I want the high-top cleats," she pleaded. "I don't want to hurt my ankles."

She had me at hurt. I didn't want my baby hurt either. So, we got her a pair of high-top cleats that had Velcro fasteners around the ankles for added support.

"BrayLee has some just like this and they are great!" she gushed as we checked out. She was so happy.

So happy, however, was not the term you could've used to describe my husband. "BrayLee's dad wraps her Velcro straps with athletic tape because they aren't that great," he sighed.

47

And within two tournaments, BrayLee's dad was wrapping not only his daughter's shoes, but our daughter's shoes as well.

Within the next two tournaments, our daughter was begging for new cleats yet again.

Really, aside from the Velcro, they were not in too bad of a shape. The actual cleats were not worn down, the laces were still in good condition (despite the caked on red-clay notorious to softball laces), and the inserts were still fitted—despite the stinky stench.

In other words, they were still good to go. This presented us with an unfortunate situation.

With tears in her eyes she begged us to get some more. "Please! I'm not used to running and moving with high tops and the tape makes them hard for me to pitch."

My husband cut his eyes at me. I pretended to be caught up in some important text on my phone. I shouldn't have been the one to pick out her cleats. This is true. I am not disputing this fact.

And apparently, neither should my peer-inspired daughter.

So many times, we choose what we want because someone else has it, it looks cool, it's the "in" thing. Or we make choices that are uninformed or ill-thought out.

The consequences are not comfortable. In the case of the cool cleats that BrayLee apparently rocks, we were out a nice chunk of change, and our kid was uncomfortable on the field she so dearly loves.

My husband took pity on her—and truth be told, it is painful to watch your kid be uncomfortable. He took her to get a different pair of cleats, and at the next tournament, she took to the field a happier, more comfortable player.

When our choices make us tired and weary, even causing us to stumble, as the scripture says, God encourages us to take our hope in Him. He wants us to fly and run and be strong. The hope that comes from our Creator is like a comfortable pair of shoes—we can go for hours without our feet hurting.

God of Hope, we seek Your forgiveness when we make choices that hurt us and hurt others. We want to have the hope that comes from You. Be the guiding force in all things that we do. Help us to know that You will provide that hope for us if only we seek You. In Your comforting name, Amen.

-14-

The First Pitch

Throw your anxiety onto Him, because He cares about you.
I Peter 5:7

Our older daughter, Hadley, played softball until she was ten years old. The last year or so, she trained to be a pitcher. And, for the most part, she was pretty decent for our rec league. Funny thing was this: She only pitched one pitch during an official game.

She pitched batting practice and worked her tail off in our front yard, but when the coach, a very good friend of ours would say, "Had? You ready to go in?" something would stop her from nodding her head yes.

Anxiety.

Her "What Ifs" always got the better of her.

What if they hit it?
What if they don't?
What if I can only throw balls?
What if the umpire has a small strike zone?
What if I hit the batter?
What if she charges me?
What if my team doesn't back me up?

What if my mom misses the shot, and I never get on her Instagram?

What if I throw my glove and hold onto the ball?

What if ...

What if ...

What if ...

For someone who truly deals with anxiety, the *what ifs* are endless.

When you play on a team and must depend on others, it's truly hard to fully let the *what ifs* go.

But, with a lot of positive talk and assurance from us, her coach and her teammates, Hadley went in for the last inning of that season. It was the championship game and it was clear that our team was not going to win. We were very close to time expiring when Coach Sheffield looked at Hadley and said, "You wanna pitch?" She sucked in her breath, put her *what ifs*—her anxiety—out of her mind and nodded her head.

She was given five warm up pitches, all fast balls, right down the gut. The umpire motioned for the batter to step into the box and Hadley took the mound. She nodded that she received the call and then began her wind-up. She let go of the ball and hit the umpire in the head.

All the *what ifs* that had been keeping her off the mound rushed right back into her life when he, probably out of embarrassment more than anything, called the ball game.

I do have to wonder what exactly he was watching that he couldn't move out of the way. I chuckled and then I looked back at my girl. Just a moment ago, I had seen the weight of the world descend upon her shoulders. Now, I saw her do something that she rarely did: She shrugged it off.

Even though they lost the game, and the championship as well, she shrugged her wild pitch off.

A few weeks later, with the season clearly in our past, she announced that she didn't want to continue with softball. She wanted, instead, to pursue golf—she could work alone, not have to communicate with others (much) and quiet, contemplative time was actually encouraged.

It was as if the sport were made for her.

As for the *what ifs*? Well, she's still learning to shrug them off ... aren't we all? It's a good thing that God's promises, unlike game times, never expire.

Holy God who cares for us enough to take our anxiety, our what ifs, and allow us to shrug off that which causes us pain and concern and frustration, we thank You that Your promises are with us until the end of time. We also thank You that You have made us each for different things, allowing our world to be beautiful and varied in Your creations. In Jesus's name we pray, Amen.

-15-

Best of Friends and Worst of Friends

I'm sure about this: the One who started a good work in you will stay with you to complete the job by the day of Christ Jesus. I have good reason to think this way about all of you because I keep you in my heart. You are all my partners in God's grace, both during my time in prison and in the defense and support of the gospel.
Philippians 1: 6-7

Because Hadley pitched that one fateful pitch in her final softball game ever, she feels like it's not only her privilege but her right to tell her sister exactly how well, or more often, how not-so-well, she pitched in any given game.

Briley doesn't share in her sister's beliefs. Let me be clear: When she does well, she loves to hear her praise; when she doesn't do well, she doesn't even want to ride home in the same car as her sister, much less hear her critique.

In addition, Hadley doesn't like to hear her parents brag about her sister's games, but she really doesn't like to hear us criticize Briley either.

Double standard? Absolutely. For as long as there have been sisters, this standard has existed. They can dog each other all they want, but they cannot and will not tolerate anyone else, including their parents, taking a swing at their sister when they are down.

This is nothing new to sisters, much less siblings, I'm sure. When anyone speaks of sibling rivalry, the names Cain and Abel are bound to be uttered at some point in time.

I don't think that my girls can be compared to Cain and Abel (on most days). I know that normally, they only want what's best for each other, despite their screaming fits over who gets which hairbrush in the mornings. But, I know that watching the other struggle, watching the other not do as well as she could have or should have is just as rough on the sister as it is on the player.

Because of this, Hadley doesn't always attend every game that Briley plays. She'll tell you that she's tired of the ball park or wants to work on homework or doesn't want to eat ball park food, but the truth of the matter is this: Sometimes it's hard to watch your sister struggle. (I say "sometimes" because sometimes she's the one making her sister struggle.)

And with softball, or any sport really, the player could have a string of great games that are so much fun to watch or she could have one bad move after another with absolutely no rhyme or reason as to why.

Truth be told, none of us like to watch when someone else struggles. But we're not always given the choice of staying home when that happens.

It's completely easy to jump on the "Good job!" bandwagon. We all want to be a part of any successful story. But it's never easy to stick around when the going gets tough, so to speak.

When Paul wrote his letter to the Philippians, he started with great encouragement, saying that the One who started good works in them would be continuing that good work. What better way to encourage someone who is down? Sure, you're having a bad day, but don't fret. God's goodness resides in you and He is not planning on removing it any time soon. His grace is abundant and isn't going anywhere.

Thank goodness because our bad games will, at times, outnumber our good games.

Our Father who has started good things in us, thank You for the encouragers who see the good and push us to do better. We ask for forgiveness when we fail to see the good in ourselves or in others and ask that You give us grace enough to find glimpses of You in all things. In Your good and graceful name we pray, Amen.

-16-
Run, Turn Left, Run Some More

Many nations will go and say: "Come, let's go up to the mountain of the Lord, to the house of Jacob's God, so that He may teach us His ways and we may walk in God's paths!" Instruction will come from Zion and the Lord's word from Jerusalem.
Micah 4:2

When Briley was just starting the game of softball, she started off with t-ball, as most prodigies do. She and thirteen other little four-year-olds were on the "Little Bruin" team, coached by my friend, Heather Hawthorne, and me. Some of these kiddos had older siblings and had a basic knowledge of the game. But, some of these Little Bruins had no idea what they were doing on the field or why.

This became evident when we played follow the leader around the bases. One Little Bruin, who we mistakenly thought had a rudimentary knowledge of the game, eagerly said, "I'll lead them, Coach!"

We lined all the little runners up at home base and let our leader hit a ball off the tee. The others would then follow her as she ran around the bases.

Only, she didn't run around the bases. She ran around—that part she did well. The bases? Well, they were just minor details in her game of follow the leader. They ran to center field, to the corner of left field, to the pitcher's mound ... at one point they even ran outside of the field and around the fence.

Coach Heather and I tried hollering at them, "No! Go to first base!"

But, if one doesn't know first base, our yelling was in vain.

We tried to catch up with them, but let's be honest here: Fourteen four-year-old girls all in one line is not the easiest thing to catch, especially if we don't know where they plan to go next.

When they returned to home and deemed that they had just scored fourteen points, Heather and I had to try a different approach. We would lead them. (Novel idea, huh?) Heather, who's in much better shape than I am, was the leader. At each base, they would stomp on the base and holler out the name of the base. I stood at home and encouraged them.

They each crossed home plate and were greeted with a "Great job!" and a high five from their lesser-in-shape coach.

"Fourteen runs again!" one Little Bruin proclaimed.

"We're the best team ever!" another proclaimed.

It seemed that they were all excited and felt confident that their first hits off the tee would result in fourteen runs.

Then one Little Bruin raised her hand, the look on her face told us that she wasn't as enthusiastic about running the bases as her teammates were.

"So," she started, crossing her arms across her chest, "We just have to run and keep turning left? That's all there is to it?"

Aside from being completely impressed that she knew her left from her right, she did have a point. That's really all there is to it: Run, turn left, turn left, turn left, then go home.

I'm sure the girls thought the way of their original leader was much more fun—who wouldn't want to race through the dug outs, outside the fence, over the parking lot logs and around the pitchers mound before coming home. But, if you want to actually score, the pathway is simple: Run, turn left, go home.

God's ways are pretty simple as well. Go up the mountain of the Lord, let Him teach us His ways, and then walk in His paths.

Our welcoming Father, who loves to see us come home. Thank You for making Your ways known and easy. Forgive us when we go off the path You've set in front of us and continue to give us instructions over and over again. Your way is easy, and You've called us to walk it daily. Thank You for making that our task. In Your loving name we pray, Amen.

-17-

I Missed It

... Because even though I am absent physically, I am with you in spirit. I am happy to see the discipline and stability of your faith in Christ.
-Colossians 2: 5

I cannot even recall why I wasn't at the one-day tournament in Muskogee. As is usual, when Brian and I have to divide our time between our girls' activities, I usually go with Hadley and Brian goes with Briley. I'm sure that this was the case on this particular Saturday, but I honestly cannot recall what Hadley and I had going on.

When we are split like this, Brian and I use up no less than twenty-nine thousand, four-hundred texts between us, keeping each other apprised of the goings on of our girls.

Whatever Hadley and I had going on finished quicker than the tournament, so we were home when I got the text:

Briley just hit a grand slam homerun

There was no punctuation at the end. There was no picture. There was no other explanation.

59

I muttered the word *What* aloud and then texted my husband back:

Nu-huh

Then I put my phone down, and I think I did laundry. I am always doing laundry, so this is a safe bet.

The next text I got was a picture of the scorebook.

OHMYGAWSHSHEDIDJUSTHITAGRAND
SLAMHOMERUN!

If the picture is to be believed, of course. My husband is a crafty guy. He's full of jokes and loves a good prank. While I trusted him with my own life and the lives of our children, I just wasn't quite sure I trusted him to text me the truth about our baby's first major—MAJOR—hit.

So I called him.

The call went to voice mail.

That man! Who did he think he was to just drop news like that and then dismiss my call. The nerve.

Then a call from a number I didn't know. Accidently, I answered it. Shoot!

Me: Hello?

Brian: You rang?

Me: Why didn't you call on your phone?

Brian: It's dead.

Me: Which is what you will be if you've lied about my daughter's grand slam homerun.

Brian: (chuckled) Why would I lie about that?

Me: You're warped in that manner.

Brian: No lie. She hit it.

Following that call from a seemingly-random phone, I was tagged no less than sixty-seven times with pictures of the hit, my kid running, her team greeting her, the score book, and a selfie from a four-year-old (because she's a cutie).

I was absolutely thrilled for my baby girl. I was absolutely crushed that her sister and I weren't there. It struck me then: I won't be able to be there for all the good things that happen in their lives. I would, however, be beyond excited that their discipline, their stability, their faith in Christ Jesus will lead them to great things.

She may never hit another grand slam homerun, but she will continue to do wonderful things—hopefully loving things. And I will know that those things come from God.

Giver of all good things, forgive us when we are absent and when we doubt the good in our lives. Give us a peace that the good things You have given to us will continue to come to us and will be passed on because we have faith in a generous savior. In His name we pray. Amen.

-18-

A Little Nod

Then I heard the Lord's voice saying, "Whom should I send, and who will go for us? I said, "I am here; send me."
Isaiah 6:8

It was during one of her first tournament games that my daughter, standing on the mound, nine-years-old, shook off a pitch.

Apparently, the coach had called for a pitch, the catcher had relayed the call, and my daughter shook her head to indicate a negative response.

I leaned to my husband and whispered (because I didn't want people to think the little rebel was mine if this was a mistake), "Did she just shake her off?"

My husband chuckled and said, "Apparently." He wasn't so quiet about it, though.

Eventually, they both revealed to me that her shaking off the pitch was actually her indicating that she didn't understand or see the call. According to Briley, it was that she couldn't see the call; the catcher was positioning her hand behind her glove.

"Whew!" I commented upon hearing the explanation, "I'd hate to think you blew off the coach."

She laughed and agreed with me that it would be a move that would land her on the bench quickly, regardless of how well she was throwing.

I've never seen her shake off a pitch since. She's a good pitcher—don't mistake what I'm about to tell you with my not thinking she's great (because she is, no bragging; just fact!): But if all she threw were fast balls straight down the gut, eventually she'd never do her job. If she stuck with the pitch that was the easiest for her to throw, the other teams would eventually regard her games as batting practice and would probably run right over our team.

She needs the coach to see ahead to the next batter, to look back and see how this batter has performed in the past, and to know Briley's strengths and weaknesses and set her up to do her job for her team.

We, too, have a great coach who gives us great calls. Unfortunately, we shake off God's calling way too frequently.

Teach Sunday School. (shake) But I'm too busy and little kids don't like me.

Stop and give that man some money. (shake) No way—he'd use it for drugs.

Don't buy that purse; donate to the shelter. (shake) But it'd go great with that cute dress.

Make an extra casserole and share it with your neighbor. (shake) I'm already up to my elbows in cream of Ritz cracker soup; I can't possibly do another.

Reach out and invite her to your home, your church, your group. (shake) But, I don't want to seem like one of those pushy Christians

Give up yourself and follow me. (shake) Yeah, but, I'm pretty comfortable where I am.

What if we nodded our heads in agreement to what God calls for us instead of shaking our heads and offering excuses? How different would our world be?

His children would be clothed.

His people would be fed.

His praises would come from the mouths of people all over.

Our lives would be filled with glory and blessings, more than we could handle. If only we just give our God a little nod of our head ... maybe even mutter, "Yes, Lord. Here I am."

All-knowing and all-loving Father, who sees not only what's behind us, but what's before us, give us a faith to trust You and answer a confident "Yes" when You call. Provide us with a trust in You that is unshakable so that when the mission is set before us, we don't hesitate to nod our heads in agreement with You. In Your name, Amen.

-19-

Of Dance Moms,
or Finding Your Clothing

Strength and honor are her clothing; she is confident
about the future.
Her mouth is full of wisdom;
kindly teaching is on her tongue.
She is vigilant over the activities of her household;
she doesn't eat the food of laziness.
Her children bless her; her husband praises her...
Proverbs 31: 25-28

Because we couldn't sign the girls up for soccer or t-ball until they were four and dance had a class for two year olds, I started off as a dance mom. I had the shirts and the hats and the bags that all declared I was a dance mom. No offense to my dance mom friends, but I (and my daughters) were not cut out for the dance life. My girls are interpretive dancers at best, and you just can't teach that kind of dancing, regardless of how many hundred-dollar costumes you buy.

We quickly moved on to soccer because the girls actually could start that in the fall and our rec league only had t-ball in the spring. I needed something to keep them busy and out of my house all of the seasons. Hadley

65

danced when she played goalie. (So the dance classes kinda paid off.) Briley broke a child's leg by accidently kicking his shin guard. (Apparently not understanding it's a no-contact sport.) Despite the fact that I had a soccer patterned chair and had contemplated getting a soccer cling for the back window of my minivan, we abandoned soccer for softball. My soccer mom life was short lived as my dance mom profession.

Again, I created a Pinterest board with softball shirts, bedding, cookie cutters, jewelry and anything else that popped up when I searched softball. I threw myself into being a softball mom.

In the off-season, I dabbled in being a theater mom (too much drama for me), a basketball mom (too fast paced for me), a golf mom (love it still!), a Science Olympiad mom, a book club mom, and a homeroom mom (shudder!). I fought the good fight and won; I was never a cheer mom. (No offense cheer moms—I'm sure you're lovely … even if you live in Texas.)

With the many "mom" titles I bore came color-coded calendars for the girls and synced-up Google calendars for Brian. I organized more snack lists than there are Little Debbie variations. I bought all the support gear that came across my desk. I drove to sell and eventually deliver fund raisers (although, thankfully, my husband does the lion's share of this). I took my role as Whatever-Season-It-Was Mom very seriously, sacrificing nutrition, sleep and sometimes personal hygiene to make it work.

Through it all, though, I hoped that my daughters and my friends didn't lose sight of the fact that I was not only a mom but a daughter of the living God.

It was and is so easy for me (and probably most parents) to get so caught up in their children that we fail to take care of ourselves. And most of that self-care can be encompassed when we take time to be with our Heavenly Father.

Unfortunately, you won't find God-time on my color-coded calendar. You won't find Him in my carpool rotation. You won't find Him on my snack schedule. I take for granted that He's there—He cannot say the same about me, though.

Recently, our older daughter, Hadley, synched a daily alarm on all of our phones. It arrives with the tiny little ding of any other announcement on my phone. Each day, the message is slightly different, but still similar:

God Loves You.
Have you Prayed Today?
What are you thankful for?
God is calling you to great things.
Jesus is your best friend.

I may be vigilant over the activities of my household, but I want God to be vigilant over the activities of my life.

Heavenly Father, Thank You for the blessings of being a mom, of watching my kids grow and become Your children, of having a child lead me to You. When my life gets too busy, call me back to You and show me the ways in which You would have me be. In my brother's name I pray. Amen.

-20-
The Uniform That Stays Together

*Therefore pick up the full armor of God so that you
can stand your ground on the evil day and after you have
done everything possible to still stand.*
Ephesians 6:13

When Briley got her first official competitive team
uniform, I cleared out a drawer in her room for her two
tops and one pair of playing pants. She had an additional
pair of practice pants, an orange belt and orange socks.
When a tournament was over, I'd wash the uniform and
place it back in her drawer. When the next tourney
started up, we knew exactly where the uniform was.

Easy!

Simple!

Nothing to it!

Her competitive team changed and she now had
three tops, three bottoms, three socks and two belts.
And some weekends, we'd go through all of these
combinations.

Then, she started school ball—which included two
shirts, two pants, two different pairs of blue socks and a
blue belt.

The drawer became too small and Briley became lazy in putting her things away. On more than one occasion, she wore mismatched black socks instead of blue because she was convinced that her blue socks were on the school bus. I'm not sure why they'd be on the school bus, but I thanked God right there that I didn't have to ride on a school bus with a softball team that apparently took off their smelly game socks.

Keeping track of all the uniform pieces became a chore. If we had only had to launder the uniform, it might be a different story. If we had only one team to keep track of, it might be easier. If we (and I use that pronoun lightly) would put the uniform where it belonged when we weren't using it, I know for a fact, it'd make life easier.

Do we do this with our God-time as well? Do we sometimes misplace our devotional time with extra time in front of the television or at the mall or sleeping in? Do we give up our time of prayer because it doesn't fit into our busy schedule?

I know that I am guilty of doing just that. I have a specific place in God's plans. He's called me for wonderful things, but if I don't take the time to listen to Him, to visit with Him, to study His messages, then I am not doing my part as the body of Christ here on earth.

Keeping track of my time with my Maker shouldn't be difficult. I should carve out a portion of my time daily to give to Him. I should make sure all of my actions are a reflection of the loving God who doesn't toss us to the side until the next game.

I shouldn't cast my thanksgivings off when I've been blessed. I shouldn't drop my concerns on the floor, never taking them to the One who can comfort me. I should keep track of all my time, devoting it to Him who keeps track of every last hair on my head.

As for keeping track of Briley's uniforms ... well, black socks don't look that bad with a blue uniform.

All-knowing Father, thank You that I'm never out of Your mind. When I cast You off to the side, failing to keep track of the devotion and praise that You deserve, You still love me. That's a devotion that I cannot even fathom ... yet You love me more than I can know. Help me to carve out the time for You that You deserve so that I can represent You clearly to those I encounter. In Jesus' loving name I pray, Amen.

-21-
A Rebel By Any Other Name

Every scripture is inspired by God and is useful for
teaching, for showing mistakes, for correcting, and for
training character, so that the same person who belongs
to God can be equipped to do everything that is good.
2 Timothy 3:16-17

I was thrilled that the Oklahoma Rebelz picked up Briley after her first team disbanded. (Imploded is a more accurate description.) I was not thrilled with the name, though.

Let me start with a history lesson first: Oklahoma is not considered a part of the South because we were Indian Territory during the Civil War, thus we didn't take official sides. But, we have just enough southernism (pretty sure that's a word) in our state that the word "rebel" takes on a negative connotation when you see it superimposed on a confederate flag on the front of a pick-up.

The word, when used in the south or in Oklahoma, conjures up visions of racism and disrespect, bringing up a bittersweet history that's not at all even close to being settled.

71

Yet, I found myself yelling, "Go Rebelz!" just the same as I had yelled, "Go Blizzards!" or "Go Slug Bugs!" a few years before.

Softball names don't always make sense, y'all.

It still bothered me some because I wanted my kids to be associated with nobleness and leadership and, well, winning.

The good news is that this team had the winning part down. As far as nobleness and leadership, I couldn't really complain either. Our coaches were top notch and the other families were really lovely and welcomed us into their fold. But still ... rebels?

Funny thing about rebels sometimes—a lot of times—rebels have birthed the most important parts of our history.

Think of Martin Luther King, Jr., who rebelled against a wrong against humanity. He said that God has created all men equal and that we all have a right to dream and grow and exist together in peace. Without his rebellion, we might still have some very archaic practices against humanity.

Think of Martin Luther, who rebelled against the ancient Catholic church fighting to restore the Bible to a central place in Christian doctrine, and to emphasize the importance of grace in making salvation possible for all. He is essentially the start of the Protestant faith; protest, being the root word there. I think he'd be pleased with the way Protestants and Catholics can now work side-by-side for the Kingdom of God.

Think also of Jesus Christ. He pushed aside the old, binding practices of believers and brought to life a new and beautiful message: God is love.

Jesus fought the Pharisees, the scholars, the tax collectors. And just when it seemed as though he'd lost his battle, he rebelled against death, beating it for all persons who believe in Him, offering us eternal life ... made possible by His rebellion against what was "normal" at the time.

One of my favorite friends, Christine, calls herself a heretic, or a religious rebel; she even has a blog by the name of "Devotions from the Resident Heretic." From her blog: *A heretic is one who seeks God for herself, not being content to follow the rules and regulations of an established religion, but to test the boundaries and verify that indeed what she is being told is truly the voice of God rather than the rhetoric of man.*

And there, my friends, is my peace. I want my kids to rebel. I want my kids to seek God for themselves. I want my girls, including the girls on Briley's team, to test boundaries and for each of them to find the voice of God for herself.

I want to, from now until my last breath, cheer, "Go Rebels!"

Oh Jesus, who has taught us to seek a loving God, I thank You for your rebellious acts on earth so that all persons can come into a personal and intimate relationship with You and the Heavenly Father we all share. Allow us to listen for the voice of Him who created us and not the voice of man. In Your loving and heretical name we pray, Amen.

-22-
Confidence In Our Countenance

*We live by faith and not by sight. We are confident,
and we would prefer to leave the body and to be at home
with the Lord. So our goal is to be acceptable to him,
whether we are at home or away from home.*
2 Corinthians 5: 7-9

I remember the very first game pitch that Briley threw that wasn't a strike. No sooner had the ball left her hand did she holler out, "Oh, shoot!" This was actually her very first pitch ever and it left her hand as if it were rocketing for the moon. Oh, shoot, indeed.

Shouting out when the pitch doesn't go your way, though? This is not a good habit for a pitcher to develop.

At the time, it was cute. She was nine-years-old, she was playing in the recreational league in our city, and the batter swung at the big, yellow ball that was probably eighteen inches above her head. She missed, but she gave it a valiant effort. They both did.

All the mommas, daddies, grandparents and friends in the stands laughed. It was pretty comical: A pitcher who told her pitches, a batter who swings at anything, and a dug out and field full of coaches who just dropped their heads and shook them, half to hide the laughter and half to hide the frustration.

The next pitch was an exact replica of the first pitch, complete with an "Oh, shoot" moment, the wildly swinging bat above the batter's head and the ducking umpire.

The third pitch though, found our little pitcher saying, "YES!" as she hurled one down the gut. The batter swung and missed muttering a "dang it" knowing that she was now out.

Technically, in the most basic of all forms, this was a strike out. My daughter, however, could not take credit for it, despite her running to every single one of her teammates in the field (including the center fielder) for a high five. She even stopped the batter as she slunk back to her dug out and hollered, "Good job swinging!"

Her confidence level was through the roof—if we had been playing in a dome, that is. And her pitching improved as a result. It didn't improve a whole lot during that particular game, but she did stop shouting "oh, shoot" when her ball didn't do as she wanted it to.

This is what happens when we become confident in our faith.

We stop grumbling when things don't go as we planned; we know that it's not the end—we'll get more pitches.

We stop swinging at everything that comes our way; we know God has great plans for us—perfect pitches are coming our way.

We stop shaking our heads, we stop kicking the dirt, we stop sighing in desperation.

Instead, we hold our heads high.

We speak confidently and encouragingly.

We continue to use the gifts and talents that God gives to us, knowing that He's the coach and we're just the players.

Walking by faith can be scary, but so can walking by sight when we only see our shortcomings and our failings.

Heavenly Father, who gives us confidence as His children, forgive us when we hang our heads, mutter our disagreements and feel as though we've failed. Give us courage to try and try again, knowing that You've got a game plan, if only we walk by faith and trust in that which we cannot see. In Christ our brother's name we pray, Amen.

A Tale Of Two Kids

We have different gifts that are consistent with God's grace that has been given to us. If your gift is prophecy, you should prophesy in proportion to your faith. If your gift is service, devote yourself to serving. If your gift is teaching, devote yourself to teaching. If your gift is encouragement, devote yourself to encouraging. The one giving should do it with no strings attached. The leader should lead with passion. The one showing mercy should be cheerful. Love should be shown without pretending. Hate evil and hold on to what is good.
Romans 12:6-9

Hadley just got up from my computer. She searched **this** document for two different words: Hadley and Briley. She knows that this is a devotional book, specifically for sports families, namely softball. She knows that Briley's softball requires a lot more time than her activities. She also knows, now, that Briley's name is used (so far) almost double that amount of times her name has been used.

And, because she's a teenager, Hadley threw in the zinger that goes right to a momma's heart: it was clear to her that I love Briley way more than I love her.

I wanted to be sarcastic and fire back some comment about her breaking the momma-writer code. Whichever kid gives her momma more fodder for her books wins and gets all the love.

But I didn't.

Instead, I offered her comfort by listing off all the many, many talents that she has that don't involve softball.

Hadley's an amazing golfer. She doesn't like the competition, so you won't see her on the LPGA in the future, but she is encouraging to her teammates (all of whom are younger than she is) and really enjoys being out on a course without any distractions other than a tiny, dimpled ball.

Hadley also has a sharp eye. Last year she won four ribbons at the county fair for her photographs. She entered five categories—it was almost a sweep. She was so empowered by this that she saved up her money and bought herself a fancy, schmancy camera. No more iPhone images for her, except for selfies on Instagram, of course.

She's quite a wordsmith as well. As a freshman, she made the staff of the high school magazine. Hadley blogs, she writes for pleasure and for credit, she digs deep in her research and she produces some of the most amazing things I've ever read. (I am an English teacher—I've read a lot.) And rarely does she use the words *a lot.*

Hadley used to play softball and was a pretty decent little player despite her one time on the mound; she preferred first base. And even though this book is about my "other" daughter (B r i l e y ... that way it can't be searched in the document) and our softball life, that doesn't mean that Hadley's loved any less.

It's a hard truth to buy into, though.

As parents, we have to model ourselves after God. We have to acknowledge the many gifts and talents of our kiddos. We have to place value on them and encourage them and lead them down a path that takes them to the place God is calling them to. For some of us, that path involves a softball complex. For others, a football field or a musical auditorium or a stage or a kitchen or a hiking trail or a newsroom ...

Allowing God to direct our paths as parents will ultimately allow God to direct the steps of our children as well. Hopefully, maybe, our children will see that is the greatest love we can give to them.

Will this chapter make up for the fact that [insert Hadley's sister's name] is used more in this book? Probably not—she's fourteen, after all. But hopefully it will let her see that her talents are God-given and noticed.

Father God, you love us and lead us in a way that is so good. It's hard as parents for us to do the same thing with the children you've given to us. Hold us steady on the path you want us to follow, give us strength when we are weak and show yourself in the many gifts and talents we and our kids display and give to the world. In the name of your only son, our Lord, Jesus Christ, Amen.

-24-
Empty Ice Chests

*You've been filled already! You've become rich
already!
You rule like kings without us! I wish you did rule
so that we could be kings with you.*
I Corinthians 4:8

"Anyone want this last bottle of water?"

Regardless of the outcome of any given tournament on any given tournament weekend, my husband will ask this question as we load up the car to head home. How or why we always end up with only one bottle of water is unknown to me. Sometimes, someone takes the last water from the ice chest, and sometimes the water stays in the increasingly warming water. Often times it's forgotten until the next tournament.

On more than one occasion, my husband and I have frustrated each other over the empty—or nearly empty—ice chest. I'm of the school that we dump it out as soon as we get home and let it dry. He's settled firmly in the camp that the emptying of the ice chest can wait, especially if we get home late. On more than one occasion, he has even let it sit in the back of the hot vehicle until the next time we need it. Both of us too stubborn to do it the way the other thinks it needs to be done. I'm sure we're the only married couple who play these silly little games with each other.

On a good day, which generally means we've finished late in the tournament and don't have significant plans early on Monday, I might dump the ice chest myself without any grumbling about having to get the laundry started. Or, I might get laundry started and let the ice chest begin to mold in the back of the vehicle. And sometimes, if I'm really lucky, Brian will dump the ice chest without my having to ~~nag~~ ask him repeatedly.

But, typically, when we arrive home, the girls will drag themselves into the house, calling dibs on the showers and consequently the hot water, while Brian and I unload the vehicle and quibble about the ice chest.

In the grand scheme of things, we have it so wonderfully. We've just spent a weekend watching our child be physically active. There are parents who often spend their weekends praying over their impaired child.

We've just spent a weekend eating nachos and cheesy fries and other greasy and bad-for-us food. There are families who go to bed with their stomachs grumblings.

We've just spent the weekend paying exorbitant amounts of money in gate fees, food fees, equipment costs, team fees, gas money, sun block and endless amounts of sunflower seeds. There are parents who wonder how they can pay the electric bill for the month.

Our girls go in and take hot showers, slip into clean pajamas and crawl into nice comfortable beds. There are families who squeeze themselves into cars or cubicles in shelters or tents illegally pitched in a concealed field.

Brian and I quarrel over emptying the ice chest. We are royalty compared to the families that go days—lifetimes—without drinkable water.

My prayer is to regard the empty ice chest as a sign of how richly God has blessed us … like royalty, we are, like kings. The dirty laundry is a sign that we have robes as brilliant as Solomon's. The empty water bottles remind us that He leads us beside still waters.

Like royalty, indeed.

King of kings, You give us daily reminders that we are blessed, that You have given us a life that is rich beyond our measure. Forgive us when we fail to thank you; Forgive us when we fail to see the blessings for the assumed burdens. Extend Your grace to us when we fail to extend it to those who are truly in need. In Your son's name we pray, Amen.

-25-

Immediately, If Not Sooner

When the angels returned to heaven, the shepherds said to each other, "Let's go right now to Bethlehem and see what's happened. Let's confirm what the Lord has revealed to us." They went quickly and found Mary and Joseph and the baby lying in the manger.
Luke 2: 15-16

"Go! Go! Go! Go!" our coach shouted to the runner who had just slid into second, ahead of an overthrown ball. Keeping her eyes on the coach, who windmilled his arm, she ran into third and then ran on to home. For those of us watching the entire field—or scanning the entire field—we quickly saw that this really was a race between our runner and the defense, specifically, their control over the yellow ball. Our team's spectators joined in the coach's chanting of "Go! Go! Go! Go!"

Their team's folks joined with their team and shouted, "Home! Home!" guiding their defense's throw of the ball.

All in all, from both sides of the field, it was an amazingly awesome play. The girls were both prepared and ready for that exact situation and executed it flawlessly. When the dust cleared at home plate, and the run had been awarded and both coaches shouted out their "Good jobs," I have no doubt in my mind that they were speaking to both teams. The fans of both teams stretched out their necks to offer their "Wows" and "Nice plays" not only to the players but to their counterparts on the other teams as well. And the players were even congratulating one another even though one team didn't gain an advantage because of this.

It was clearly one of the better plays of the entire tournament.

And just what made it so amazing to all involved? I like to think it was the immediateness of the actions.

If even one of the players on the field had faltered in her actions or delayed her action or questioned what she was doing, the outcome would have been much different. Instead, of a chorus of cheers for a job well done, we'd have heard a field full of grumblings. It was in the precision, the timing and the willingness of the players to do what they were called to do when they were called to do it.

This is not unlike the way in which Christ became human and entered into our world.

The softball play started with an error—an overthrow. When Jesus took on His human form, he came to correct the errors of the world.

At the time of Christ's birth, shepherds, those hard-working men of the field, were given clear instructions from the angels to go and seek the baby King. And they did. They didn't pause. They didn't ask for clarification. They didn't ask for the instructions to be repeated. The scriptures are clear on this: They went quickly and found Mary and Joseph and the baby Jesus.

We are called daily by our Creator, our Heavenly Father, to continue the ministry to Christ: To reach out to the lost, the lonely, the hurting and the needy. Sometimes the instructions are clear and the path is made straight—a homeless family needs clothes immediately after we've cleaned out our closets or an elderly neighbor needs a pick-me-up on the same day our kiddos decide to deliver some hand-picked flowers to her.

Sometimes the instructions are not so clear and we pray for guidance and light to shine as we seek to be God's hands and feet to a still-hurting world.

Whether our calling is clear or needs clarity, one thing is certain: we're called to immediate action. We're to believe that we are equipped to do that which God has placed before us and we're to do it without question. When we immediately seek to answer God's call, as the shepherds did on the night of Jesus's birth, our actions will flawlessly fulfill the ministry of Christ.

Heavenly Father who gives us salvation through Christ and who calls us to continue His ministry on earth, we ask for Your calling to be clear and our response to be immediate. Remove any doubt from our minds and enable us to be swift in our actions, just as the Shepherds were on the night of Jesus's birth. Move us to be faithful in serving Your children on earth, just as our Brother, Jesus the Christ. It's in His name that we pray, Amen and Amen.

85

-26-
Shiners and Other Trophies

[Joseph said to his brothers,] *You planned something*
bad for me, but God produced something good from it, in
order to save the lives of many people,
just as he's doing today.
Genesis 50:20

Briley came home one afternoon from a hitting session with an older pitcher. A wild pitch had caught her on the shoulder. The ball stitches were prominent on her bruised shoulder.

She came home another time with a ball-shaped bruise on her calf. And still another time, she came home with a mid-back bruise—complete, again, with stitch-shaped bruises.

The best trophy, however, was the shiner and cut she got on her right eye. There were no stitches, but I was afraid she'd need stitches. (She only required a butterfly bandage.)

"What happened?" I gasped seeing my baby's beautiful face marred by a black eye and an abrasion just to the outside of her eye, slightly above her cheekbone.

"Coach hit me," she grinned. I knew there had to be a story behind this if she were grinning. I also knew that our coaches loved each girl as his own and would never allow any of them to be harmed in any way. "But, I got him back," she followed up.

Apparently, while fielding, she shifted her body too late and the sun blinded her just as a pop fly landed on her sunglasses, breaking them and cutting her face. Coach, when seeing she was okay as evidenced by her rocketing the ball right back at him hollered, "Use your glove and not your face, Davis."

Later on, she hit a ball right back to him and sprained his thumb. "Use your glove, Coach," she casually commented when he shook out his hand.

Injuries, while not desirable, are inevitable, especially if an athlete is giving her all to the game or activity she loves. When they happen, she has two choices: She can let it define her and bring her down, or she can shake it off, learn from it and continue on with the game.

Briley moves on from her injuries so seamlessly that when I ask about them, she recalls so many more than I do. As her momma, it makes me feel inadequate that I can't remember them all, but it's a testament that she doesn't let them define her.

And while I think that a cut (almost) to her eyes is a significant injury, in the grand scheme of things, it's nothing.

The lesson we learn from Briley's injuries and from Joseph's brotherly betrayal are that our injuries don't need to be game-stoppers. If Briley had given up on softball after her first injury, she would've never made it past t-ball.

So, what if Joseph had decided to just wither away in his cell and give up on his faith? How very different his story would've been! Instead when Joseph saw his brothers, the ones who betrayed him, he opened his arms wide, accepted them back as brothers and proclaimed the goodness of God to make all things beautiful.

To be able to see that God is constantly looking to make something good from the bad that happens in our lives is truly a gift and a blessing. Our injuries no longer define us; instead, they provide a stage for our God to be glorified.

O God, our God who works to make all things good for us, thank You. Thank You that You keep us from harm. Thank You that You give us good things. Thank You that You know us so well that Your glory is able to shine through us. Forgive us when we don't acknowledge the goodness that comes only from You. Free us to be a shining trophy of Your glory. In the name of Jesus Christ, our savior, Amen.

-27-

T-Shirt Addiction

But the Lord said to Samuel, "Have no regard for his
appearance or stature because I haven't selected him. God
doesn't look at things like humans do. Humans see only
what is visible to the eyes,
but the Lord sees into the heart."
I Samuel 16:7

I have at least eighteen softball mom t-shirts. Eighteen. When you consider that my friend, Christine, has evening gowns that she bought on sale and has yet to wear, eighteen softball mom t-shirts doesn't seem like such a big deal.

But when you consider that I bought two t-shirts online at a tournament and I already had them in my closet, then I might have a problem. I mean, one *was* a different color so there's that.

It's as if I don't want anyone at the softball complexes that we visit to mistake me for just anyone who might be watching random girls playing softball. I want them to know that I'm there in the official capacity of *Mom*.

89

Hypothetically, I could wear a different softball mom shirt to every single game during a tournament even if we played the maximum number of games, and I would still not run out of softball mom shirts.

I've worn these shirts when I'm not at a softball event as well. I've worn them while grocery shopping, while walking, while out to dinner with the family and while out to dinner with friends. They are not just for softball tournaments, that's for sure.

Funny thing is that not once has anyone ever stopped me, inside of or outside of a softball complex and said, "Oh! Does your daughter play softball?"

They have, however, stopped me when I've been running to the fields with an ice pack and asked, "Is your daughter hurt?"

They have, upon hearing me yell, asked, "Is that your daughter?"

They have, upon seeing me in a laundry room with a pile of dirt-caked pants, asked, "What position does your daughter play?"

But never has anyone said, "Oh hey! Your shirt! You must be a softball mom."

The truth of the matter is that my actions speak for themselves: People can tell by my deeds that I'm a softball mom. They don't need a t-shirt to tell them what my cheers and actions clearly show them.

In addition to my eighteen t-shirts, I also have four softball caps and almost a dozen pieces of softball jewelry.

These items, because they are not emblazoned across one's chest, are not as easily noticeable.

At one particular tournament, I was decked out in a softball shirt, bracelet, earrings, flip-flops and cap. It was overkill to say the least, but I looked pretty cute if I do say so myself. I cheered loudly, supported our team and enjoyed the mild spring day.

Then I saw another softball mom. She was also sporting a shirt, earrings, necklace, tennis shoes and a slightly different accessory: a cap that declared she was a *softball b!+@#.* She screamed just as loud, supported her team just as much and seemed to be enjoying herself … as long as her team was winning.

She seemed to be a spoil sport. Her hat may have been the most honest thing I'd seen all day long. Immediately, I disliked her.

Was this all because of her hat?

My reaction gave me pause. I want my outsides to match my insides. When people look at me (or hear me), I want them to see what's in my heart; in the case of my softball regalia, I want them to see a mom who's proud of her daughter and who wants to be as supportive as possible. My actions should be enough to speak that message. My outside should line up with that but shouldn't have to advertise my intentions. More than that, though, I want to look at others as God sees them. I don't want to make a snap judgment based on their outsides. I want to know a person from the inside out.

All-seeing God, who knows us better than we know ourselves, help us to be honest in our behaviors and our appearance. Forgive us when we judge another of Your children based on the outside. Draw us closer to them, hoping to find the goodness You've planted within each of us. And let everything we do, everything we say, everything we wear be a reflection of You so that someone may come to know You better. In Your precious and holy name, Amen.

-28-

In The Stands

Know this, my dear brothers and sisters: everyone
should be quick to listen, slow to speak and slow to anger.
James 1:19

One particular tournament weekend, my mom was with us and thus I was not able to be at the entire tournament (which would quickly become the norm in the sandwich generation). Brian and Briley left early that morning and we would follow later on that afternoon once we knew how we were seeded in the bracket.

We arrived in time for the three o'clock game and met up with the team as they took to the field, having home advantage. Briley was in the circle. I parked my mom, in her wheelchair, next to the dugout, which provided her with sufficient shade to keep her cool and unsunburned. Brian, already engrossed in the game two pitches in, was seated with the tablet, keeping stats for the team just a little way away from my mom. He barely knew we were there.

I stood with her for a while then eventually took a seat in the stands. I sat beside a family I hadn't seen before and in front of an older gentleman I'd seen at one other tournament at that same complex.

Briley struggled with the first few pitches before coming alive and quickly taking out the next three batters. As our team jogged off the field, the gentleman behind me, tapped the family next to me and asked, "Are you with Rebelz?"

When they answered that they weren't, I started to mention that I was, but since I was wearing a Rebelz shirt, I thought he might ask me next. He didn't, though.

"Do you know anything about that little pitcher?" he asked, continuing to direct his questions to the family beside me.

They admitted that they'd played Rebelz a couple of times before and had come up against #27. "She's a good little pitcher," the mother added.

My chest puffed full of pride, I wanted to enter the conversation and let them know that she was my kid and, while her daddy was the main driving force behind her success, I had been a softball pitcher myself until I was about twelve years old. Before I could begin my brag-fest, the gentleman burst my bloated pride.

"Is she always that inconsistent?" he asked.

I sucked in my breath, tempted to tell him that this was her fourth game, our other pitcher was injured and, while we had a pick-up player, our coach was just more confident in her abilities. Inconsistent? *Whatever.* The first batter was left stranded at first, the second batter struck out on a full count and the next two batters were three pitches and done. Maybe she was tired. Maybe she was doing it on purpose to throw off the other team's offensive plans.

"I really can't remember," the other mom answered. I liked to think that she said this because she wouldn't want someone dogging her player without any defense.

The only conversation during the next half of the inning was my inner dialogue. Maybe I should say something. Maybe I should demand to know exactly who he was and what authority he had to decide my kid was inconsistent. Maybe I wouldn't say anything but I'd passively call him out on Facebook or my blog. I said nothing and texted Brian, asking who he was. If he were one of our fans, I was going to say something for sure. If he weren't, I probably would say something just in a very snarky way.

At the end of that inning, Brian turned to me, looked behind me and shrugged his shoulders. Without even asking why I wanted to know, he focused yet again at the game in front of him, our daughter warming up. I chose to say nothing.

Nine pitches. Three batters. That half of the inning was quick.

I heard the gentleman behind me chuckle to himself. "Well," he said, nudging the woman beside me on her shoulder, "I guess I spoke too soon. I bet I see her pitch at the college world series in a few years."

What a knowledgeable and kind man.

Oh God of good humor, thank You for the gift of self-control. Thank You for ears that listen and mouths that shut. Thank You for placing us in situations that teach us humility and grace without causing us too much embarrassment. Remind us daily that You are in control, and we are a reflection of You to all people. In Jesus's name we pray, Amen.

-29-

Poker Face

Hide Your face from my sins;
wipe away all my guilty deeds!
Create a clean heart for me, God;
put a new, faithful spirit deep inside me!
Psalm 51: 9-10

When Briley first started pitching, she made it really easy for the batters and the umpires. For every strike that she threw, she would grin and holler out a little, "Yeah!" For every ball that she threw, she would grunt disapprovingly, sigh really big and sometimes stomp her foot. She'd usually go through this ritual before the ball even hit the catcher's mitt.

Her pitching coach and her team coach both had long, serious conversations with her about this. She was a good pitcher, she had excellent potential, but if every batter knew when to swing or not swing, she might as well hire out her services for batting practice because she wasn't going to have a career as a game pitcher for very long at all.

She would have to work on her poker face. When she threw good pitches, she'd have to look just as stoic and serious as she did when she threw junk balls. If she

97

were going to make noises as she pitched, she'd have to make the same noises for every pitch.

Who knew that she'd spend just as much time practicing her face and her voice as she did practicing her pitches?

There were many afternoons, evenings and weekends that Briley and Brian would set themselves up in the front yard, working on her pitching faces and her pitching noises. I could always tell when she'd accidently grunt and grimace at a bad pitch or grin at a good pitch. She'd holler out "Dang it!" when she'd slip up. It was going to be a long road.

Her love of the game eventually won out and she mastered her game face. Regardless of whether or not the pitch is spot on or completely off, her face never changes. If they're up by six runs or down by seven, her face is the same as it was for any other game.

And this worried me.

Briley has always been the joker of the family. She likes to play pranks (and often ends up being the butt of her own jokes). She likes to laugh and have fun and is often the life of the party—even when there isn't a party. Her friends' parents would bring her home from sleepovers and play dates and comment two things: Briley was a fun kid, and they were exhausted by her visit.

Seeing her stone faced in the circle was unnerving for me.

Seeing her stone faced in the circle and her pitching improving by strikes and strikeouts was amazing.

Seeing her confidence in herself and her abilities skyrocket make me smile because I knew my kiddo was using her talents to the best of her ability.

She still threw clunkers and she, on rare occasions, walked a girl or threw a pitch that was hit and ended up too far out in right field, but her face never changed. After those pitches, she'd conference with the coach—both of them talking equally to each other. She had mastered her game face, but that didn't mean she shouldn't or couldn't acknowledge her poor pitches. She knew when she messed up; she'd talk to her coach about how to make it better next time. Even when she was taken out of games, she'd talk to the coach. There was a lot of head nodding and positive exchanges, even as she'd hand the ball over to her relief.

When we mess up, it's easy for us to keep a stone face and hope no one else saw. But the truth is that even if no one else saw, our Heavenly Father is fully aware of those times when we fall short of His expectations for us.

Still, God creates a clean slate for us, a pure heart, a new start. He sees beyond our faces and into our hearts When that forgiveness is given and grace is poured onto us, we can break our poker face and smile at our renewed spirit.

Grace-giving Father, thank You for the gift of forgiveness. Thank You for the promise of a new life in You. Thank You for loving us, despite seeing our sins and knowing that we often try to hide them from You. Forgive us when we fail to be the child You created us to be. In our Savior's name, Jesus Christ, we pray. Amen.

-30-

Freedom!

Therefore, stand firm and don't submit to the
bondage of slavery again.
Galatians 5:1

We had a rare, free weekend.

Fall ball had ended; off season hadn't started. We didn't have Science Olympiad, Battle of the Books, mid-term tests, choir concerts, orchestra concerts, youth group trips ... we had nothing going on.

When Sunday evening rolled around, I wouldn't have piles of laundry to do, we wouldn't be racing to finish homework, we could watch *America's Funniest Home Videos* in real time while eating a real meal made in our own kitchen.

Freedom, indeed.

On Thursday of that week, the girls asked what we had going on for the weekend, and we announced, officially, that we had nothing planned. This excited even them.

Thursday evening when we returned from Olympiad meetings and hitting lessons, we sat down together for dinner and made our plans for our free weekend.

There was a new restaurant in a neighboring town we'd heard great things about. A fun museum just south of us was hosting their Free Family Weekend. We wanted to invite some friends over for game night. And while we're at it, we should just make it a front-yard food night complete with grilled burgers and a movie. Briley had been wanting to have her friend over, and Hadley had been wanting to do a Netflix binge on *Pretty Little Liars*. The lawn needed mowing, and I couldn't tell you the last time I cleaned out the refrigerator. My mom wanted to make a Sam's Club run, and this would be a great weekend to do family pictures for our Christmas card. And I was way behind on my writing—in fact, I had two deadlines that were on the verge of being missed. Plus, it'd been a month of Sundays since we'd been to church as a family.

Before we were even finished with our Thursday night meal, we'd planned about five days' worth of stuff for our two-day weekend.

We laughed about our excessive plans, and then, like fools, we packed our weekend to the brim and exhausted ourselves silly. Sunday evening found us putting *America's Funniest Home Videos* on pause while we scrambled to get homework completed, hurried to finish laundry, rushed to pack lunches and fussed as we cleaned out the vehicle from the busy, busy weekend. The girls packed their backpacks and fell into bed forty-five minutes past their bedtimes.

Brian and I looked at our calendars to sync up who would need to take the kids or Mom here and there and when we'd be together for dinner and when we'd fend for ourselves. Our next free weekend was five weeks away.

We sighed in unison. How silly (some might say stupid) we had been to fill our weekend so full. How gluttonous even. How was it that we were allowed to be adults making decisions that take away our much-needed down time?

I imagine that God looked down on us that evening and shrugged His shoulders as if to say, I gave you a good gift—a free weekend—and look what you did. Silly kids.

But, it's what we as humans do, right? We're given good things and then we neglect them, we fail to care for that which our Creator has entrusted us with. Perhaps in deep, dark times, we thank God for the miraculous gifts he bestows upon us. It's easy to see God when He shines in our dark times. But in the light, when things are going well, we too often divert ourselves back to slave hood, failing to look for our Heavenly Father, the very one who set us free through His son.

Silly kids, indeed.

Our God, who is as constant as the air and the ticking of time, forgive us when we fail to see You and the good gifts You lay before us. Grant us eyes that look for You first, in good times and bad, and the wisdom to accept Your gift and use it to glorify You. Through Your son, both human and divine, Amen.

-31-

And The Answer Is ...

But happy are you, even if you suffer because of righteousness! Don't be terrified or upset by them. Instead, regard Christ as holy in your hearts. Whenever anyone asks you to speak of your hope, be ready to defend it.
I Peter 3: 14-15

Long before Briley ventured into the travel softball realm, Hadley tried out for a competitive team. She was a fairly decent pitcher and had a gun for a right arm. Her bat wasn't too shabby either. When Brian and I asked her if she wanted to try out for this particular team, she answered a weak "yeah" and shrugged her approval.

Because we are constantly having to divide our time between our very busy kiddos, I took Briley to a birthday party while Brian took Hadley to the try-outs. He texted part-way through and said Hadley was running as if she wanted to be dead last. I texted back that running wasn't her strong suit. In fact, she hated it.

She's not talking to the other girls either, Brian texted. I answered back that she was an introvert in every sense of the word.

Finally, Brian sent one last text: There's no way she made it.

I sighed and answered back that it was too bad, but ... I had heard of another team with try-outs the very next week. Maybe she was just having an off-week.

When we got the call that Hadley had not made the team, just as Brian predicted, we were heartbroken as parents. It's never easy to tell your kiddo that they aren't good enough for a particular activity. We braced ourselves for the tears and heartache. I put on a pot of water to make some homemade macaroni and cheese to comfort my little baller, and then together, we went to her room.

"Hadley?" I said as we entered, "Honey, I'm so sorry, but you didn't make the team."

She looked from me to her daddy and back to me before nodding her head and saying, "Okay."

Okay? That was it? Where was the emotion? Where were the tears? Why wasn't her little chin quivering like it always did when she was upset?

She continued to hold our eyes with her own and then asked, "Are you okay?"

The truth was the Brian and I were clearly more upset by this rejection than our kiddo was. In fact, she might not have been upset at all. I tried to coerce her into crying. I tried to convince her that she would feel better if she got sad about this. I got nothing.

Finally, she said, "Softball really isn't my game. I prefer to work alone. I don't like running. I don't like having to depend on someone else to catch the ball and do the right thing. It's just not my thing. Sorry."

Sorry—bless her heart. She shouldn't have to apologize for being herself.

"Do you know what is your thing?" I asked her as I slipped my arms around her, pulling her close to me in a hug.

"I think I'd do well with golf." There was actual hope tangible in her statement.

Wouldn't we all be happier if we could know what we like, know what we don't like, and find hope in rejection? When someone tells us no, wouldn't we be more serene in looking for the thing that can be a yes for us instead?

Maybe our yes comes from trying harder and continuing down that road. Maybe our yes comes from changing our pathways and starting a new venture. Maybe our yes comes from seeking counsel and allowing ourselves to wait.

But always, our yes comes from knowing Christ Jesus and the hope He freely gives to us.

Our hope is in Your spirit and Your power, Jesus. When the answer is no, we ask for comfort and direction and hope that You have better things in store for us if only we continue to walk with You down whatever path You lead us. With hearts and minds full of Your grace we pray. Amen.

-32-
When Mom Yells

[Preparing for exile] *Listen! The sound is getting louder, a mighty uproar from the land of the north; it will reduce the towns of Judah to ruins, a den for wild dogs. I know, Lord, that our lives are not our own, that we're not able to direct our paths. So correct me, Lord, but with justice, not in your anger, or else you will reduce me to nothing.*
Jeremiah 10:22-24

I had been yelling at the girls to come and empty the dishwasher for ten minutes. I got no response. In frustration, I marched back to their rooms, banged on their doors and summoned them to the hall. Without any further word from me, they both emerged from their respective rooms, proclaiming their innocence.

"I didn't even hear you!"

"It's my turn to do the top of the dishwasher."

"I'll wait until she gets done."

"No, you go first..."

The fight was on.

Sometimes it seems as though my voice has been blocked from their auditory systems.

Then, there are times when they can't help but hear me. Case in point: I whispered to my husband that I'd like some ice cream and both girls, who had been in their rooms with headphones on came running to the kitchen with their own sweet, frozen requests.

I get it—a child reaches a certain age and selective hearing is the best a parent can hope for.

Unfortunately, their listening is not always a good thing. Or maybe, it's my talking that's not always a good thing.

At one of Hadley's basketball games, Briley and her friends had already played and were goofing around on the bleachers behind me. Aside from the officials being incredibly inept, there was one particular girl on the opposite team who was the embodiment of a poor sport. She fouled for the sake of fouling, she often threw herself on the court and began crying when things didn't go her way and she argued with the officials, often times calling them names and not getting a technical. I leaned into a fellow basketball mom and said, "That number 22 is a prissy."

The game continued, but my words kept ringing in my ears. I probably would have told #22 and her parents that she was being a priss; I'm not necessarily shy like that, but I didn't know her back story, why she was like that or what she was like off the court. Still the words resounded through my mind just as loudly as they would have echoed through the gym.

That's because my younger daughter and her friends were sitting three rows up from us chanting, "Twenty-two is a prisssssseeeee! Twenty-two is a prisssssseeeee!"

107

Embarrassed and ashamed are the two best adjectives to describe me as I made my way up to them to shush them. What could have been a quick apology and a request that they stop.it.right.now, turned into a quarter-long explanation about why my actions were in no way acceptable and completely wrong in every way.

The girls peppered me with "Why did you say it?" and "Do you even know her?" and "What makes her that way?" And as uncomfortable as it made me to admit my wrongdoings to a group of first grade girls, I'm sure that it was immensely better than having to explain my actions to #22 or her parents.

In the gym that January Saturday, I learned that I'm more than grateful that I don't have to direct my own paths—that God can lead me where I need to go. And when I need correction, it will be just. Calling a child prissy might be most justly corrected by a group of precocious eight-year-olds.

Father in Heaven, who created us to be the best yet watches us become our worst, forgive us. When our own minds and thoughts direct our actions down a less-than-desirable way, swiftly and justly redirect our steps so that our actions—including our words—demonstrate Your mighty power, compassion and grace. In Jesus's precious and beautiful name we pray, Amen.

-33-
Book Worm

But the land will be full of the knowledge of the
Lord's glory,
just as water covers the sea.
Habakkuk 2:14

After a tournament wherein we did a lot of sitting around waiting for the next game, Hadley decided to take along her books to the next tournament. She wanted to make sure that she'd have something to do in the down time, and she wanted to stay up on her schoolwork. It was April, after all, and school was beginning to wind down.

The next tournament was better planned and we didn't have a lot of down time. That didn't stop Hadley from setting up herself up in her camp chair, right behind home plate, and digging out her various books. She had a book review due for English, and they were in the process of finishing up *The Outsiders* as well. She pulled out her science book on occasion to work on vocabulary and to finish up her semester study guide. She had a book she was reading for Battle of the Books and she brought along her American History book because social studies is her favorite subject.

109

She would, on occasion (when the crowds got loud), bring her face out of her books and look at the field. She knew when her sister was pitching and when she was hitting and made an effort to watch her sister's efforts. Mostly, though, she was oblivious to what was happening in the ball park.

"C'mon, now!" a team dad razzed her, "Are you really going to read a book instead of watching the greatest game there is?"

She glanced at him, giggled and returned to her book without being phased.

"Okay," he continued, "Since it's so interesting, let's make a deal: If you finish that book before the game is over, I'll give you $10."

Brian and I cautioned him that she was a pretty quick reader, so he amended his offer.

"And you have to tell me about what you just read."

Without raising her head, Hadley murmured her agreement.

Shortly before we took the field for the last time in that game, Hadley triumphantly shut her book and said to the deal-maker, "Let me know when you want my report."

Between games, Hadley and he talked about the book she'd just finished. She filled him in on the protagonist and antagonist. She let him know her takeaway about the book's relevance to today's society. She gave him background on the author's previous works and works in progress. She was in her element talking about books and being academic-y.

The fellow softball parent listened intently and asked questions. His interest seemed genuine, and he didn't hesitate to pull out his wallet and offer her the payoff. Then he pulled out his phone and took a picture of the book. He admitted that he'd never been one for reading, but he had a genuine desire to read that book now.

I know my daughter. She likes challenges, she likes books, and she likes money. Her intent was never to convince him to read the book. Her intent was to read and get paid to read.

Wouldn't it be something if we were all so passionate about sharing our faith? Wouldn't it be something if, when we met someone who challenged us, we rose to the challenge and demonstrated our faith in such a way that that person wanted to know more and felt compelled to find out more on his or her own?

Daily we meet people who seek to know more about God and who yearn to hear the good news that comes with knowing Jesus Christ. Rise to the challenge and live your life in such a way that people want to hear what you have to say about our great God.

Father, thank You for the gifts needed to rise to the challenges we face. Make clear those in our encounters who are ready to hear the Good News that comes from You and from Your son, Jesus. Strengthen us so that we can share our faith in such a way that others can't help but long to know You better. In Your Amazing name I pray, Amen.

-34-
Strangers In The Dug Out

Be happy in your hope, stand your ground when
you're in trouble and devote yourselves to prayer.
Contribute to the needs of God's people, and welcome
strangers into your home.
Romans 12: 12-13

"We had a new girl on the team," Briley announced after a day full of softball games.

"A new girl?" I questioned, noticing someone new in the dug out but not knowing who she was.

"Well, I think so," Briley said, unsurely as she took off her cleats and stunk up the car. "Coach said she was a pick-up girl."

"Pick-up player," Brian quickly corrected.

"Yeah," Briley confirmed. "Pick-up player. Some of the girls didn't talk to her. Apparently she played us before on a different team and they were poor sports."

I smiled. This was probably 9-year-old code for *they beat us.* "Did you talk to her?"

"Yeah," she said, her smile evident from her seat in the back. "She's a good player. I hope we pick her up again."

I was proud of her for not jumping on the no-talking bandwagon and looking beyond a previous loss to the talents and gifts this stranger had to offer. A few seasons later, Briley would find herself as a pick-up player for a team we'd never played before. They needed a pitcher and had seen her throw. They contacted Brian and asked if we were free for a one-day tournament. We were and made the two hour trip for Briley to pick-up with them.

Prior to our arriving at the complex, Briley admitted that she was nervous. "What if they don't like me? What if I have an off-day?"

We reassured her that even if they didn't like her or if she threw only balls, it was one day and a temporary situation. "You're not always going to be on a team with just your friends—especially if you go on to play school ball or even college ball."

Turns out the girls loved her. Briley was on and the team handily won first place in the tournament. They gave Briley the game ball and she had all of her new friends sign her tournament shirt. She also got three offers to pick up with other teams, and we have maintained a good relationship with two of the coaches, checking in with them and working out with the team when we're in their area.

Briley's fears were unfounded.

The fear of the unknown often times keeps us from stepping out of our comfort zones. By nature, I am introverted. I'd just as soon sit away from the crowds at the ball park, cheer for my team and walk quietly to my car. My fear, though, would deprive me of knowing the other softball families that I have come to know and love.

Briley, if she had given into her fears would have never picked up with the team. She wouldn't have

113

developed friendships and working relationships if she had said she was too scared to step into a strange dugout.

There are people who extend fellowship and friendship to strangers—to me, to my girl, to my family. For those people I am grateful.

When I extend that same grace, when my Briley extends that same grace, we are extending the hand of God on earth. We are offering the companionship of Jesus to our brothers and sisters. We are being a welcoming and warming smile to a stranger, hoping to become friends.

Gracious and loving God, who first invited us to fellowship by giving us Your son as fellow man on earth, thank You for people who are willing to be a welcoming face to strangers. Give us the courage and strength to extend Your grace to all of those we meet, but especially to strangers who may be searching for a friendly face. In the comforting name of Christ Jesus we pray, Amen.

-35-
"Battling"

The calm words of the wise are better heeded
than the racket caused by a ruler among fools.
Ecclesiastes 9:17

She wore a shirt emblazoned with her daughter's number and name as well as the team logo. She had the softball hat, shoes, jewelry ... she was decked out with her softball regalia. Of course, so was I, so it wasn't her appearance that stood out. Instead, it was her voice.

She had a very distinctive voice. It was deeper than the average female voice and had just a touch of gravel to it as if she had just gotten over a cold or was on the verge of catching one. And at the end of every cliché she threw out for her team, she lifted her voice just a very, tiny bit so that her cheers sounded as if she were maybe asking a question? (See? You just did it, didn't you? Did it again ... right?)

"Battle, baby, battle!?" she hollered into her megaphone about thirty times before the batter ever got into the box.

"Eye on the ball—keep your eye on the ball!?"

"Swing for the fence, #4, swing for the fence!?"

"You got a piece. You got a real good piece!?"

115

"Straighten it out, baby, straighten it out!?"

"Battle, baby battle!?"

"This is your field! Your game! Your win!?"

Her loud clichés seemed to never end, just as her constant yelling. Toward the end of the game, I looked around to find that no one else was even attempting to cheer other than the obligatory, "Woohoo!" along with applause at a good play.

On the one hand, I really appreciated her excitement and enthusiasm for the game and for her team. On the other hand, though, well … my other hand was covering my ear.

I don't want to seem like a spoiled sport (because we did lose this particular game), but her constant and loud barrage of softball clichés was a distraction. On more than one occasion, I found myself staring at her, sitting just to the right of home plate, instead of watching the game. I was equally fascinated, wondering how she breathed (it seems as if she didn't take a breath between chants) and annoyed at both her and me because I gave more of my attention to her instead of the game. In fact, the folks sitting around me seemed to have more to say about this 40-year-old sound machine than they did about the eleven girls and one batter on the field.

Maybe that was part of her goal; maybe she wanted to distract us and the other team just enough that our heads were not in the game. If so, well played, Loud Woman, well played.

As the game ended, I found myself more concerned with where she was and what she was doing. Did she also have casual conversation featuring only clichés?

Was she somewhere sucking oxygen, trying to refill her lungs? Did she stand around saying nothing at all because she had said it all, needing to rest her vocal cords for their next game?

My annoyance continued until our next game, when my focus on the Rebelz returned.

How easily we are distracted, huh? Instead of enjoying my daughter, enjoying our team, cheering for the good plays and shouting out encouragement for the not-so-good plays, I listened to this woman's endless shouting and exasperating clichés. It's not always just the woman who distracts us, though.

How many of us waste hours on Facebook or Twitter or Instagram? How many of us stare at the coupon clipper in line ahead of us at the supermarket? How many of us choose to binge on Netflix instead of binging on God's word? Or serving others? Or testifying to the goodness of our God through our words, our deeds, our actions?

The world is full of loudness. We need to find a way to keep our focus on the calm that is found in our salvation.

O Lord who calmed the sea and quieted the storm, speak gently to us in the noise of the world. Call us back to You over the racket in our lives. Drown out the clatters and the commotions that keep us from making disciples in Your name. Through Christ our brother we pray, Amen.

-36-

Face Off

As a mother comforts her child,
So I will comfort you; in Jerusalem you will be
comforted.
Isaiah 66:13

My friend, Jan, is a football mom. Her son warned her at the beginning of every football season that if he were to get hurt, she was not to step foot on the field. She could check on him after the game. He made this very clear every year right up to his Senior year.

I distinctly remember him standing next to her saying, "If I'm ever hurt, I do not want to see my mom's face while I'm on the field."

Up to that point, he had never been hurt, and she'd never had to test herself in that situation.

But, that late October game found him lying still on his back on the thirty-yard line. Jan, sitting in the stands, looked at her husband who cautioned her to let the trainers to take care of him. "They know what they are doing," he chided, implying that she did not.

She glanced at her younger children who seemed to be oblivious to their brother's injuries.

Jan knew she had to go to the field. Grabbing her bag, she sped down the bleacher and pushed her way past the knelt cheerleaders and went straight to her injured son ... right after digging a Halloween mask from her bag and pulling it over her head.

She arrived just as they loaded her son onto a stretcher. He looked at her and said, "Mom?" with a very child-like voice.

Jan replied, "Yes, honey, I'm here."

"Why the mask?" he asked as they moved swiftly toward the ambulance.

"You said you didn't want to see my face."

Lance, Jan's son, turned out to be just fine. He was pretty bruised up and sat out for two weeks with a concussion, but he was well enough to laugh about his mother in a werewolf mask on the field. He was able to play his last game of his senior year. Jan sat in the stands with her werewolf mask in her bag ... just in case.

As parents—particularly mothers—there's very little we can do to keep ourselves from our children when they are hurt or are in trouble or are in need of any little thing. We ache when we cannot comfort our child and help to make things better. Moms will move heaven and earth to get to their hurting child.

If we, as human parents, are that anxious and excited to be with our children, how much more so is our Heavenly Father to have us near Him?

More importantly, how often do we push God away? I don't know that any of us reading this devotion right now would do this intentionally, but are there ways in which we toss him to the side, preferring to listen to the noise of the world instead of looking for the face of our Messiah?

The good news is this: God will not be wearing a mask. When we seek Him, whether we are in the midst of trouble, hurt, strife, in good times and bad times, He has promised to be by our side, offering comfort, support, grace, forgiveness and love. Always He offers us love.

Try, today, to seek Him in all aspects and all times of our lives so that with Him, we can live the life He is calling us to live.

Father, forgive us for pushing You away and failing to seek Your presence. Thank You for choosing to be by our sides and not hiding Your comfort from us. Continue to be near us, guiding us down the trail You've prepared for us. In Jesus's name we pray, Amen.

-37-

Lessons? Again?

From now on, brothers and sister, if anything is
excellent and if anything is admirable, focus your thoughts
on these things: all that is true, all that is holy, all that is
just, all that is pure, all that is lovely, and all that is
worthy of praise. Practice these things: Whatever you
learned, received heard or saw in us.
The God of peace will be with you.
Philippians 4:8-9

"She has lessons? Again? Didn't you just have practice last night?" a friend asked my husband as he and Briley rushed away from youth on Wednesday night to her pitching lesson.

She did just have practice the night before. She'd have practice again the next night and hitting lessons in two days. It was time consuming, but we took great strides to ensure she had other activities, such as youth group, in her life. Plus, there wasn't one practice or one lesson or one softball related activity that Briley didn't love wholeheartedly.

"These are lessons," Brian explained. "Practice is different."

121

Those who are not involved in the same activities as you often times don't understand the differentiation between similar activities. Practice was with the whole team, run by the coach, preparation for games. Lessons were individual, private, honing the skills that she, personally, will be expected to have when practices and games roll around.

"And she doesn't get tired of it all?" my friend questioned Brian.

"Nope," he smiled, "she's said she loves it." And the truth is that Brian loves it just as much.

"Well," my friend smiled, "as long as she loves it and remembers us when she's famous..."

Because she loves it, she also spends her time outside of lessons and practices sharpening her skills. She pitches almost daily; she hits off of a tee, from a spinner and soft-toss with her dad; and, she watches old DVR'd College World Series games, noticing who pitches in what way and whose swing changes in which games. To give way to a southernism, she's ate up with it.

Isn't that usually the way it is with things we're passionate about? Prior to our having children, I couldn't buy enough Longaberger Baskets. I have another friend who loves Rustic Cuff bracelets so much that she buys them just to give away as well. And, some would argue that the reason I'm not a size 8 is that I have an unparalleled passion for chocolate. (I cannot argue with that at all.)

How fabulous would it be for us, in all of our time and activities, to "practice" being children of God?

What if we left church on Sunday mornings and re-read that day's scripture lesson?

How would our lives improve if we not only told people we were Christians but showed them with our interactions with the poor, the sick, the hungry and the needy?

Instead of practicing our Candy Crush game, wouldn't it be wonderful if we practiced those things that are true, holy, just, pure, lovely and worthy of praise?

The world we know would be profoundly improved if we were to take the lessons of Christ to heart and practiced them with our whole being.

God, our great and inspiring teacher, remind us daily of the lessons you've taught us and help us to put them into practice whenever and however we can. Forgive us when we become lazy and choose instead to follow the ways of the world. Gently nudge us in Your ways so that they become the only way we know to live. In the name of Christ, Amen.

-38-

Girly Girl

You are the one who created my innermost parts; you knit me together while I was still in my mother's womb. I give thanks to you that I was marvelously set apart.
Your works are wonderful—
I know that very well.
Psalm 139: 13-14

I have two daughters. They are two years apart. I had hoped that being born so close together would allow them to have common interests and friends. Like many things in motherhood, I was wrong.

One child would wear yoga or work out pants and a t-shirt for everything: school, movies, church, laundry day, holiday parties and pictures. Everything. The other child would wear only the best clothes. She would want lots of frills and the latest trends. She'd even take a change of clothes to events in order to look cute *and* fresh.

The yoga and t-shirt child has no interest in make-up. She will, on occasion, allow her sister to put some mascara on, but will, almost as quickly, rub it right off—not wash it, rub it. The frilly girl has to be face checked at the door every morning to make sure she's not going to school looking like a cross between a Vegas show girl and Tammy Faye Bakker's long-lost love child.

The no-make-up child wears a towel on her long hair for at least an hour because she doesn't want to do anything to her hair and the towel gives it a wind-tussled look that she can live with. The mascara-for-miles child wants elaborate 'dos that are worthy of a royal coronation and not a typical middle school day.

The wind-tussled girl likes wearing her Birkenstocks and Chaco sandals, sometimes year-round, and the more understated the shoe the better. The daring 'do girl wants heels and boots and straps and glitter and glamour.

Clearly, Brian and I have a girly-girl and a, well, non-girly-girl.

Much to the surprise of many of our friends and even some of our family, on the weekends, our girly-girl wears cleats and slides in the dirt. Our non-girly-girl usually has her nose stuck in a book.

When you see Briley coming off a long tournament, with dirt caked on her face like the foundation we won't allow her to wear, you'd never guess that she'll be sporting a sea-foam green dress with strappy sandals to school the very next day.

You would never guess. But, God wouldn't have to guess; He'd already know. In fact, before Briley was even a dream of ours, God knew she'd be a paradox—an athlete and a frilly female. Before we prayed long and hard for Hadley, God knew that she'd be passionate about reading and learning and comfy clothes.

On most days, the girls battle as if they are prizefighters in Vegas. On most days, I wonder where my dream of them being besties went. On every day, God knows exactly what each of us is feeling. He made us for the lives we are living. He made us to be reflections of Him in a world that desperately needs hope that can only come from Him.

He knows which outfits will end up on Briley's floor and which will end up as her outfit of choice. He knows which books will carve a place in Hadley's brain and which will be quickly dismissed. He knows which mornings I will lose my ever-loving mind because of their sisterly bickering. He knows ... because we are His creation and have been formed by the Master Creator. We are His light, His body, His uniqueness is His world.

Creator God, how wonderfully You have made each of us. You have created us to be strong, passionate, compassionate, loving and beautiful. You have placed us in this world knowing full well what our actions will be, what our decisions will be, what paths our lives will take. Just as You formed us before we took our place in this world, continue to form us to be what You need us to be. In the name of Your son, our savior and brother, Amen.

-39-

Who Needs Water?

When you pray, don't pour out a flood of empty
words, as the Gentiles do. They think that by saying many
words, they'll be heard. Don't be like them because your
Father knows what you need before you ask.
Matthew 6:7-8

In Oklahoma, we have two temperatures during the summer: Hot and Hotter. It was one of these hotter summer days when I found myself single parenting. I don't remember where exactly Brian was, but I had to get Briley to softball practice by myself.

This really doesn't sound as daunting as it is. Brian loves softball and always has, so he has taken over, I'd say 99% of all things softball. My 1% is showing up when I can, wearing a cool softball-mom shirt and cheering.

As practice time approached, I had Briley loading the minivan with her softball paraphernalia while I stood around and asked if she needed items that apparently were worthless as they resulted in her rolling her eyes and scoffing at my obvious incompetence.

We bid adieu to my mom, who initially relished the thought of living with her granddaughters after her stroke, but I think she's come to cherish her beloved alone and quiet time as the days go by.

I dropped Hadley off wherever Hadley needed to be dropped off. I ran my one errand and then Briley and I headed to the fields.

"Do I need to help you unload?" She shook her head no.

"Should I stick around?" Again with the negative action—since it was a hotter day, I may have audibly surrendered a *whew*.

As I put the car in park, I turned, proud of myself for accomplishing, by myself, everything that normally Brian and I both would do. "Anything else?"

She shook her head yet again. Maybe this was part of her practice ritual. Maybe she was always this quiet. But still, I was used to her chatting and her silence was a little bit sad to me. Then, she blurted out, "My water!"

Fail.

On a hot, hot, hot day, I had forgotten the water. "Dang it!" I hollered. "I'll run back home and get your water bottle." It was probably still sitting on the counter where I placed it so we wouldn't forget it. Brian knew her practice routine. I'm sure he'd never forget. And really? It's not that hard! I should've remembered—it's hot, my baby would need hydration.

"Don't go all the way back home," Briley advised. "When Daddy forgets, he just goes to Quik Trip and gets me a water."

When Daddy forgets... Ah! Beautiful words! I wasn't alone.

Just a few moments in the heat, unloading her equipment, had me already sweating. How could I forget the water? Even with his routine firmly in place, how could Brian forget the water?

The answer is easy. We're human. We're busy. We're forgetful.

Our Heavenly Father, though, He's divine. He is attentive to our needs. He remembers us and supplies what we require before we even know about it ourselves.

On the hottest of days, He remembers to refresh us ... and, just like our earthly parents, He likes when we talk to Him.

Ever-giving Father, who is generous with our needs, thank You. Thank You for loving us and giving to us what we need. Thank You for loving us and listening for us to speak even when we are silent. And thank You that You are divine, yet made Your son to be one of us, saving us from sin and death and bridging Himself to You and Your glory. In Your name we pray, Amen.

-40-
Florida Or Bust Or … Bust

What do workers gain from all their hard work? I
have observed the task that God has given human beings.
God has made everything fitting in its time, but has also
placed eternity in their hearts, without enabling them to
discover what God has done from beginning to end.
Ecclesiastes 3:9-11

It was only January, but we were already marking up the summer months on our family calendar. The Rebelz would be going to Florida for the National Tournament the third week in July, Hadley would be going to Kentucky for a mission trip to Red Bird Mission the fourth week in July. And then Briley, if she made the USSSA Elite team, would return to Florida the first week in August. School would start the second week. In addition, I would be teaching the second and fourth week of July during Transition Time for our incoming sixth graders at the school where Brian and I both teach. The calendar clearly wasn't big enough.

Brian and I spent many evenings, nights, early mornings discussing the logistics of our travel. Maybe he could go down early with the girls to do Disney and I would fly down after Transition Time. Hadley and I would then fly back before the tournament was over to get her ready for Kentucky. If Briley made the Elite team, Brian and Briley would fly back down, I'd drive over to

Kentucky, pick up Hadley and we'd drive down. If necessary, she and I would then drive home early and Brian and Briley would fly back after the closing game on Sunday before school started on Monday.

Brian and I would need to be ready to start school by July 4 ... just a few short weeks after school let out for summer vacation. Plus, our building was being remodeled. There was a chance we'd be moving buildings in addition to this. And? We hadn't even considered what we'd do with my mom during this time. Ideally, she'd stay with my sister, providing my sister and her family didn't have any last-minute summer traveling.

It was too much. One night as we drove to pick up Hadley from her youth group, I said what seemed to be glaringly obvious. "We can't do it all. I think Briley needs to skip USSSA this year."

There was a silence in the car that was as palpable as the stitches on a softball. "But she's worked really hard, and it's a great opportunity," Brian finally said.

"It's not an opportunity if it kills us in the process. This is not the year."

We drove in silence a few moments more before Brian confessed his agreement. It wasn't the year. The timing wasn't right. The opportunities we hoped for our daughters would still be there at a later date if they were meant to be.

That night, we talked with our family and told them that the second week in Florida just wasn't in the cards for this year. "The timing's bad," we offered to Briley as a consolation.

She was broken hearted—that much was evident—but she was also thoughtful. "So, I can do church camp?"

"More than likely," we nodded.

"What about the OU camp? Remember you said I couldn't go to Cat Osterman's camp if we were going to have to pay for hotel and food in Florida for a second week. Could we look at doing that in June? I wanna go this year with Gabby." These things that were putting a smile on Briley's face were now possibilities.

The scriptures didn't make the promise that God wouldn't close one door without opening another. What they did promise is that God provides a time and a place for everything. Some things will crush us because they don't fit into our calendars, but most things, when we take the time to look at the gifts God has placed before us, will delight us beyond measure.

Holy God from beginning to end, You have given us a time and a place for everything. You have placed on our hearts the hope of eternity and that hope makes all other things pale in comparison. Thank You for Your perfect timing. Thank You for the hope we have in You. Thank You for promising to walk with us from the start to the finish of the path You've set us on. In Your eternal and everlasting name, Amen.

-41-
Would You Like Fries With That?

God's kingdom isn't about eating food and drinking
but about righteousness, peace and joy
in the Holy Spirit.
Romans 14:17

"Are we playing at the fields by Fat Guys Burgers or Oklahoma Joe's?"

"No. It's the one by Los Cabos and Robyn's Hardens."

All of those places are some of our very favorite eating establishments.

Sadly, our tournament schedule was not just defined by the teams we'd previously met and the teams we'd yet to meet, but by the closest places to eat and how much we liked those establishments. If we went deep into the tournament and began playing without big breaks in the bracket, more often than not, our fields were designated as the one by Sonic, the one by Subway, or the one by McGaggles.

If time were really tight, and we ended up eating at the complex, we had the "chicken flatbread" fields, the "slider" fields, the "nacho" fields, and, of course, the amazing "seasoned fries" fields.

None of these choices were a healthy choice, but we have always enjoyed eating out and didn't feel a little something like a little softball tournament should stop us.

Oh sure ... we could totally have taken along sandwich fixings, fruits and vegetables, but that would have required pre-planning, and more times than not, our pre-planning consisted of making sure a ball cap was handy by the door when we zoomed out of it toward the vehicle, usually running late.

And, while we oddly associate certain fields with their closest eating establishments, when we're fixing to go to a tournament, prepping and packing food is not one of my first thoughts. But you can guarantee that we won't be two miles down the road before one of us says, "Where are we going to eat today?"

I know we're not alone in our grossly, "overused" eating-out habits. We spend a lot more time going through drive-throughs and requesting tables for five than any family should.

Irony? I like to cook. Truth? I don't like to cook for my family—they are picky and usually end up making themselves sandwiches. It's much easier on my ego and my valuable time for us to just go out to eat. Health and wellness are kicked to the side more times than not. And that's not good.

Sadly, I just described many of our spiritual habits as well. We go to our Sunday small group when our schedule allows it. We drop the kids off at youth group. We listen to praise choruses as we get ready for church. Then Sunday evening, we go to sleep only to wake up on Monday and speed through the week without considering how we need to be healthy and well in our faith.

What if I planned my quiet times with our Heavenly Father the way I planned going out to eat?

What if I only prayed the prayers when I knew exactly how God would answer?

What if I chose to sing His praise when I felt like I could sing pretty ... or when I felt like singing at all?

What if I chose to worship Him on Sunday mornings only and casually dismissed Him the rest of the week?

Like eating fast food 24/7, neglecting my faith and my relationship with my Lord outside of Sunday mornings or within the church walls, would result is a miserable existence, an unhealthy lifestyle and worthless gains.

Consider this: The Holy Spirit comes to us offering us joy, peace and happiness in a buffet format. Why would we turn down an opportunity to experience those things?

Heavenly Father, we ask that You daily send the Holy Spirit to guide us to You. We want to be reminded that You are worthy of our praise and our worship daily, regardless of where we are or what we are doing. Call us to bear Your light at all times in a dark work and to be thankful for a loving God who gives us good things to keep our spirits healthy. In the name of Jesus Christ we pray, Amen.

-42-

There's No Such Thing As White In Softball

Wash! Be clean! Remove your ugly deeds from my sight. Put an end to such evil; learn to do good. Seek justice; help the oppressed; defend the orphan; plead for the widow. Come now, and let's settle this, says the Lord.
Though your sins are like scarlet,
they will be white as snow. If they are red as crimson,
they will become like wool.
Isaiah 1: 16-18

Briley's first competitive team had great colors. Pulling from our state universities, they either wore red and white or orange and black. They looked sharp. I likened the team to miniature Sooners or miniature Cowgirls.

We are Oklahoma State fans, and were thrilled when their first day of play, they were to wear their orange and black. The next day, they wore their red (or crimson) and white. That evening, when she peeled off her uniform in the laundry room, I discovered another reason why I like O-State better: They didn't wear white pants.

It appeared that after a very windy day at a complex with dirt infields, my little pitcher, who liked to wipe her hands on her little behind before every pitch and who declared on more than one occasion that sliding was her favorite, no longer had a pair of white pants. She had a pair of brownish, reddish, tie-dye-looking pants. I guessed that we'd have to buy her a new pair of white pants after every tournament so that she could have white pants that were actually white.

Before I invested in forty-some-odd pair of pants, I took to Facebook and asked the best way to get white pants white again.

Softball moms, baseball moms, friends from all over chimed in offering their best suggestions. Oxy-clean powder! Oxy-clean liquid! Bleach! Grandma's Spot Remover! The Car Wash! That evening, I bought more laundry products than I had in all my life combined up until that point.

I rubbed, I soaked, I brushed. I spent quite a bit of time on that one pair of pants, trying to get the white back. After a trip to the car wash, we had white pants again—with just a hint of dirty spots at high-contact points.

Much like Pavlov's dog, whenever we'd get the text that we were wearing white pants, I'd groan and begin collecting quarters for the car wash.

When our time with that team came to an end, I and my chapped hands were thrilled when our new team only had black and grey pants. Clearly, the laundress had made the uniform decisions for this team. You see? When we don't have white pants, we never have to try to clean them. It was a task that I abhorred, really, before I even started.

Aren't we blessed that when our white turns dingy that God never tires of making us clean? He doesn't need bleach. He doesn't need Oxy-clean. He doesn't need a brush or a car wash or a 24-hour soak. It's an effortless gift that he offers to us without question.

And aren't we beyond blessed that the cleaning process is easy and harmless and painless? The simple act of asking for forgiveness doesn't involve scrubbing or begging or pleading. It involves a child falling at the feet of her Heavenly Father and speaking simple, truthful, heartfelt words: Forgive me.

I like to imagine that it's the grace of God's smile that washes over us as the sun washes over the dew of an early-morning outfield. And that brilliant grace brings with it a cleanliness that cannot be found anywhere else on earth ... except in the heart of a newly forgiven believer.

Bright and Holy God: my sins are great and numerous. I even sin when I fail to ask You for forgiveness. Yet, when I come to You and fall at your feet, You willingly and wonderfully let Your grace wash over me, making me clean and pure again. Thank You for the love You have for me allowing you to offer this forgiveness time and again. In the name of the one who showed us the way to forgive, Amen.

-43-

What Will It Do To MY Softball Game?

The fear of the Lord leads to life;
Then one rests content, untouched by harm.
Proverbs 19:23

I discovered the knot at the base of Briley's head while putting her hair up for one of the end-of-summer games. I moved it around a bit; it appeared to be solid.

I asked her if she had done anything to hurt herself. She said no.

I asked her if it hurt and she said only when I kept messing with it.

It was concerning ... but not concerning enough for me to do anything about it until January. That was almost six months after I discovered it. Not one of my better mothering moments.

We were at the pediatrician for another issue, and I casually mentioned it. Our pediatrician ordered some blood work, then sent us to a surgeon. One way or another, it would have to come out of her head. Maybe I should have had just a little bit more concern six months before when I discovered the lump.

As we sat in the office of the surgeon, he reassured it that he felt confident that it was nothing more than a glorified pimple. Really, though, there was only one way to find out. He could either remove it in the office, but kids didn't respond well to shots and poking around, so he recommended a one-day surgical procedure that would involve general anesthesia and a nice little forty-minute nap for Briley.

Briley's nerves got the best of her, and she began chattering non-stop about random thoughts such as if he had to shave one side of her head, would he shave the other and could he dye the tips of her hair pink while he was back there.

My husband and I checked our calendars to schedule the surgery. When Briley stopped her chit-chat and the doctor stood to shake our hands and fist bump his young patient, I asked the question that we all wanted to ask.

"What will this do for softball?"

The room grew quiet. Practices had already begun. Tournaments had already been scheduled. Our calendars had already been synced. Would this side-line our little baller?

"She can start back to playing the very next day." His reply was met with collective sighs of relief.

Obviously, we love softball and it's a really big part of our lives. But, what if we loved God more?

I'd like to say that I do love my Heavenly Father more than anyone or anything else. But, does my life demonstrate that love? Am I willing to ask that tough question before every decision or action? Am I willing to say, "What will this do for my relationship with my God?

Think about it: If that question pressed on my mind as I went on my weekly grocery hunt, would I possibly demonstrate a kindness and a patience toward the other shoppers that they may or may not give back to me?

If I asked what my bedtime routine would do for my relationship with God, would I maybe spend more time in prayer with and for my family instead of hounding them to just go to bed already?

If I pondered the possibilities that God has prepared for me before I lamented the laundry or the dishes or the dusting that never ever gets done, would I find myself being more grateful for a change of clothes and food to eat and the things and possessions that cushion my life?

The contentment we felt at knowing that Briley's softball activities wouldn't be scathed at all by her procedure is the same contentment that our Creator and Lord offers to us daily … but first we have to invite Him into our daily lives.

Father and Creator, who made us to accept Your good gifts, thank You for allowing us to lead lives that can be full of contentment as the scripture promises us. Forgive us when we fail to stand in awe of You and complicate our lives. Give to us a peace and contentment that we cannot find through any other means but You. In the name of Your son, Jesus Christ, we pray, Amen.

-44-

Crazy Family Tree

Honor everyone. Love the family of believers.
Have respectful fear of God. Honor the emperor.
1 Peter 2:17

"Ummm ... 'scuse me," a tiny little voice said as she tapped on my arm.

"Yes, ma'am?" I smiled at her, turning my head from the game for just a brief moment.

"Where's your other girl? The one that doesn't play softball?"

"Hadley?"

"Yeah, Hadley! I want to play with her."

Hadley was almost thirteen years old. Izzy was four. Their common ground was that they spent many, many hours watching their sisters play softball.

I broke the news that Hadley was at home that weekend. Izzy made a pouty face before skipping off to find another playmate.

I texted Hadley and told her that Izzy missed her. She texted back that she missed sweet Izzy as well.

As we've continued down the softball journey, Hadley has found herself playing cards with a four-year-old boy and a six-year-old boy—both bound to be future card sharks. If you ask her the rules of that game, she couldn't tell you; in fact, she's pretty sure that Weston and Eli couldn't tell you either.

Hadley's picked up Kennedy's sippy cup. She Instagrammed Noah's Rebelz rally flag. She's listened to Trinity talk about her own softball team. She's admired Ashley's accomplishments as a national cross country super star, and she's giggled at Rowan's wild and crazy hair.

At a tournament in Branson, we looked over at an adjacent volleyball court to discover that the Rebelz siblings had started a volleyball game before their sisters took the field.

I'm sure this phenomenon is not exclusive to softball. If you play on a constant sports team, you get to know the other families well, and I'd venture to guess that you even begin to love them as if they were your own family. If you are a member of any group with which you do life, you will find yourself holding tight to them in prayer and presence.

I like to think that loving each other in this manner is exactly what God pictured when He Created us to inhabit the Earth. I'd like to think that, just as we smile and get the warm fuzzies when our kids get along, God looks at us in the same way when we act out of love toward each other. We are, after all—as any Sunday School perfect attender can attest to once they learn the Creation story—family.

It's not always as pretty as the picture just painted, though. Go to the supermarket at the first of the month. Unfortunately, we don't love everyone there, least of all the checkers.

143

Hop onto Facebook and share your beliefs. Sure, you'll find some who support and agree with you, but I'd venture to guess that you'd find just as many who are able, willing and quick to tell you what's wrong with your statement. And you'll find some who will tell you how their way is so much better. (I see you nodding your head.)

This is not how God intended us to live: He has clearly called us to be a family. Sure, families fight. I'm closer to fifty than I am to fifteen and find myself still fighting with my sister. (Mostly because she's wrong.)

But, at the end of the day, we are still family.

We just need to remember that we all have the same Heavenly Father … and he wants nothing more than for us to love each other just as He has loved us. It's a tall order, but it's something we need to strive to do.

Loving and gracious Father, thank You for the gift of others, for those we know well and hold dear and those who cross our paths barely making an impression. Remind us daily, through Your love, that we were created to share You freely and generously. Forgive us when we receive good gifts but don't give good gifts to others. In the name of the one who taught us to love, our brother, Jesus, Amen.

-45-

Sleep Where You Can

[Jesus said] "Come to me, all you who are struggling
hard and carrying heavy loads, and I will give you rest.
Put on my yoke, and learn from me. I'm gentle and
humble. And you will find rest of yourselves. My yoke is
easy to bear, and my burden is light."
Matthew 11:28-30

When I was a new mom, the advice I most often got from, well, everyone, was to sleep when the new baby was sleeping. I found this difficult to follow because when the baby slept, I mostly wanted to watch her sleep. But, it was the only time I found to do laundry and cook and clean and, perhaps most importantly, to watch *Ellen*. This resulted in full-blown meltdowns (by me) about once a week when I became overly tired.

When this Momma Meltdown happened, Brian would take the baby and usher me to bed with promises that I'd feel so much better after I got any kind of rest ... even if it were a tiny little nap. He was right. I'd wake up feeling like SuperMom, ready to tackle the messiest of diapers, the wettest of bathtimes and the pickiest of eaters.

I vowed right then and there to share the same advice to my daughters when they became mothers. But, I found myself offering that advice sooner than that.

Due to late nights and early mornings, we encourage our little softballer (and her sister, as far as that goes) to sleep when they can. We promise that they will feel so much better after a little nap or snooze or doze or whatever they wanted to call sleeping. Quickly, they learned that we were right.

They've dozed in the car most often, but they've been known to catch a few winks on bleachers, under bleachers, in restaurant booths, and even on the bench outside of a grocery store.

And we're not the only ones. We've seen players and siblings (along with parents and spectators) sleep on blankets on grassy knolls and even in empty dugouts.

Being well-rested really does make a difference in just about every aspect of our lives, doesn't it? Our weariness wears us down quickly and we find ourselves useless to the world.

This is why Jesus's promise of rest is such a beautiful one. He calls to us who are struggling and carrying heavy loads, and He will give us rest. Now, this is really important: In this whole chapter, never does Jesus promise to take our struggles from us. Never does He say he'll carry the load for us. But, He does promise to give us rest.

Think about it ... regardless of where we get our rest, we wake up feeling better. Our circumstances haven't changed. Our location hasn't changed. Our lives are still the very same as they were when we first drifted off to dream. So, what has changed? We're refreshed. We're relaxed. We're restored.

Beautiful, huh? We can find ourselves lying at the feet of our savior, refreshing our minds and souls and bodies and waking to continue on our journeys.

Put on my yoke, Jesus says.

My way is gentle, He promises.

I can give you rest, He smiles.

Precious Jesus, You keep Your promises to us, and You have promised us slumber. If we walk with You, You will be gentle and humble and give us rest. You are the only one who can truly refresh us and restore us. Just as You are faithful to us in keeping Your promises, help us to be faithful in following You, rested and renewed. In Your most holy name we pray, Amen.

-46-

The Break Of Day

God is within her, she will not fall; God will help her
at the break of day.
Psalms 46:5 (New International Version)

"We'll need to leave about six," Brian proclaimed, knowing that a leave time of six in the morning would be cause for wailing and gnashing of teeth by the three girls he lived with ... mainly me. We are not morning people. Brian is very much a morning person, though.

The next morning, about five o'clock, Brian began waking us. He was, indeed, met with wailing. Hadley and I decided that we'd actually come to the next game which would allow us to sleep at least two more hours, probably three if I push the outer limits of the posted speed. I did Briley's hair, kissed her cheek and wished her luck before I dragged myself back into bed.

When Hadley and I met up with Brian and Briley later that day, I asked about Briley, very concerned that perhaps her lack of passion for mornings might affect her game, if not her attitude.

"She's doing great!" he declared. "She pitched an awesome game, and we had a good conversation."

I'd had two more hours of sleep than she did and still didn't want to function at full capacity just quite yet.

With sleep-crusted eyes still, I asked Brian if he were kidding me. He promised me he wasn't.

"Maybe she's a morning person after all," he smiled, glad that he'd have some company on early Saturday mornings.

But, the next weekend, without a tournament on the schedule, Briley slept later than all of us. So much for his theory.

"Why do you think," I asked her when she emerged from her room after the rest of us had eaten lunch, "you were so awake last weekend at five in the morning and you slept so late today?"

"Well, last weekend, I was excited and pumped about softball. Today, I know you're going to make me do my laundry."

That's a pretty accurate assessment.

Psalm 46 is talking about God's Holy city, not a softball player, but I think this scripture still works for us as His children. In the New International Version, the city is referred to as "her" and "she." So, let's do a little substitution:

Softball is within _Briley_, she will not fall; _Softball_ will help _Briley_ at the break of day.

This changes the scripture quite a bit, right? But it helps to understand how and why Briley was so willing and able to get up and moving so quickly. It totally supports her Saturday afternoon theory.

Just as God has created His Holy city, He's created us as well. So, let's do a little substitution again:

God is within _Briley_, she will not fall; God will help _Briley_ at the break of day.

This makes sense as well, doesn't it? When we invited God to be within us, He keeps us upright. He keeps us passionate. He keeps us ready and willing to go at whatever hour He calls us.

Try it for yourself:

God is within *me*, *His child*, *I* will not fall; God will help *me* at the break of the day.

Like His Holy City, He wants us to stand and He wants to help us in whatever way He can. But, first, we have to have Him living within us.

Holy God and Creator, Live within us, dwell within us, make Your home within our hearts and souls and minds. When we stand tall, let it be because of You. When we stumble, keep us from falling and when we are weary, wake us at the hard times to shine bright just as You have designed us to. Through Christ our savior we pray, Amen.

-47-

Mom versus Dad

In this image there is neither Greek nor Jew,
circumcised nor uncircumcised, barbarian, Scythian, slave
nor free, but Christ is in all things and in all people.
Therefore, as God's choice, holy and loved, put on
compassion, kindness, humility, gentleness, and patience.
Colossians 3: 11-12

Briley came home with a perfectly round bruise, complete with stitch marks, on her thigh. I asked if she wanted ice. She said she did not. Dad had already looked at it and decided it wasn't that bad.

Y'all? That bruise was black as night and covered more than half of her tiny thigh. It hurt me to look at it.

But ... Dad said it wasn't bad.

Two days later, she tumbled off of a skateboard into the grass. She hopped up, looked around and spotted me, then limped over to me complaining of hurting her ribs, head, knee, ankle, ear and tailbone. The tears she cried were real and big and poured down her cheeks like a waterfall in an enchanted forest. I kissed invisible injuries and gave her approximately four ice packs with about twenty pounds of ice. Her injuries remained unrevealed.

On another occasion, she was hit in the shoulder by a line drive right back at her. He little chin quivered, and I had to stop myself from running onto the field from the stands where I sat. Her daddy was sitting behind the backstop. She looked at him and her chin flattened out, the moistness in the corners of her eyes retreated back into the sockets and she readied herself to pitch again.

It's not just Briley that her daddy's apparent magical healing powers work on.

Hadley fell off of her bike, while Brian was right behind her. She looked at him, dusted off her knees and jumped back onto her bike. She rode the half a block, to our driveway, where I was standing and had witnessed her wreck. She took one look at me, burst into tears, dropped her bike half in the street and ran to me telling me how horribly she'd hurt herself.

What is this strange phenomenon that allows one parent to calm a child and the other parent to dissolve her into a puddle of tears?

There are other ways in which this works, too. When I ask the girls to complete their chores, they argue back with me about how it isn't fair, they've already done it once, or I've never made them do it before. But when their daddy asks them, their grumbling stays under their breath and, somehow or another, they all end up as best pals when it's all said and done.

Anyone who's ever been a parent or had a parent knows that with our individual personalities come individual behaviors. Hadley knows that if she wants to talk politics or world news, Dad's her guy. But, if she wants to talk about the latest book she's read, she comes straight to me. Briley is a daddy's girls when she wants to work out and she's my girl when we're Pinning cute hairdos. If they want someone to help them be strong, they are looking for their daddy. If they want someone with whom they can be weak, nothing beats Momma's arms.

These individual strengths (and weaknesses) are designed specifically for us by our Heavenly Father. But, He doesn't treat us any differently than He does any of His other children.

Christ dwells in us. That makes us holy, free and loved. So much so that it spills out and God expects us to share it with others in the same way He graciously shares with us.

Oh Christ who lives in and through us, thank You for making us individuals but being consistent in Your love for us. You've called us holy. You've set us free. You flow love through us so that we can be the child You've designed us to be. Forgive us when we act in a way that is not how You intended and call us to demonstrate that love to others. In Your Holy name we pray, Amen.

-48-

Not Too Early and Not Too Late

But me? My prayer reaches you, Lord,
at just the right time.
God, in your great and faithful love, answer me with
your certain salvation.
Psalms 69:13

There was a time when Briley's hitting was off. She'd have a good swing, but it wasn't timed just right. This would leave her dink-ing the ball right to the short stop, who'd effortlessly toss it to the first baseman, beating Briley and earning the out. Sometimes, Briley would swing too late, missing the ball entirely.

During this spell, she said it. Her coaches said it. Her daddy and I said it, and even her sister said it (much to Briley's disdain): Her timing was off.

Week after week, she'd meet with her hitting coach, who proclaimed, as we all knew, it's just hard to teach timing.

Each pitch is different, so she couldn't count to a certain number before swinging.

She'd have to carefully watch what pitch was coming at her, analyze its location and decide the best time to swing.

While she continued her tee work and her live arm hitting, she just couldn't seem to get the timing down. This was frustrating to everyone, but most importantly to Briley.

There's nothing that causes more frustration to a softball player than having all of the mechanics of a swing—her stance, her glance, her head, her feet—perfected yet not being able to swing the bat at the right time to make the perfect connection with the ball.

Then, as suddenly as this timing issue came on, it disappeared one weekend with a well-placed bat on a perfectly-pitched ball that flew over the head of the short stop and into center field.

"It was in the middle of the grass," Briley would later recount, and that was a good thing. Maybe her timing had returned and she'd found her groove again, so to speak.

Isn't it fantastic that God's timing is never off?

Brian and I tried for four years to become parents. We'd gone down the fertility roads and examined all of our options. We'd considered fostering, adoption, IVF, remaining childless. Many nights, Brian and I would hold tight to each other as I'd cry about the defectiveness I felt as a woman whose body couldn't seem to do what it was made to do. We prayed endlessly for a child to call our own. In March we got the call that I was viably pregnant. In November, we delivered Hadley. This didn't happen in our time, obviously. But, God delivered a child to us in His time. I can't even answer why it was a

155

struggle, but I know that now we have an answer to our prayers in the form of two silly and sweet (and sometimes sassy) sisters.

Brian tried for years to get a teaching job in my school district, but the best position never did open up—until one day it did. It's like the job was made for him.

Briley could've joined a competitive softball team a few years before we actually dove headfirst into travel ball. It would've meant two hours of travel four nights a week just for practices. We opted to wait and eventually found our place with the Rebelz.

In Psalms, as well as many other scriptures, we're promised that God has perfect timing. Our prayers reach Him and He answers us. Just as the yellow ball will eventually cross the plate and the bat will eventually strike that ball, timing is everything. And God's timing demonstrates His infinite and mighty love.

Holy Father, who hears us every time we come to You in prayer, thank You for answering us with the perfect answer but not until the perfect time. We cannot even begin to fathom our needs at every moment, but You do and You grant us an answer to our prayers granted through Your boundless love and endless faithfulness. Your timing is to be trusted above all other things. In the name of Your son, our Lord, Amen.

-49-
Allow Me To Introduce Myself

*But now, thanks to Christ Jesus, you who once were so
far away have been brought near by the blood of Christ.
Christ is our peace. He made both Jews and Gentiles into
one group. With His body, He broke down the barrier of
hatred that divided us.*
Ephesians 2:13-14

With my mom living with us and having two very
busy girls, sometimes I feel like Brian and I go days
without seeing each other. Usually Brian runs softball
and golf while I run homework. I typically do drop offs
and pick ups, and Brian does evening activities. The
spring semester is the worst.

We sometimes eat dinner around the same time as
each other, but we don't usually get to sit down together
and eat at the same time. Unless you count those times
that we stand at the stove and sample dinner together.

I've been told a million times by a million well-
intentioned moms that I need to enjoy this time with my
kiddos because I'm going to look in the backseat of the
minivan in no time at all and find it empty.

And I get that. I understand that the girls will be
grown and driving on their own in the blink of an eye. I

understand that as quick as a sneeze, the girls will be moving out and moving on. I understand that soon enough, I'll long for the days when they kept me busy and on the go. I understand all of that.

But I also understand that I married Brian because I wanted to do life *with* him, not as a co-carpooler or shared-parent. (I'd like to think that on most days, he feels pretty much the same.)

Through our daughters' experiences, I don't want to neglect the one relationship I chose to maintain for life. And that's pretty difficult.

There are some nights that we get the girls into bed, make sure my mom's in bed and doing well and then we fall in bed ourselves, exhausted and sometimes fall asleep kissing each other good night. (Okay—it happened once and we laugh about it now that we know it really happened and it wasn't a dream.)

In an effort to maintain our relationship and continue to develop our life with each other, we try really hard to have regular date nights. We also strive to have some sort of conversation daily that doesn't involve scheduling—but that's really hard to do. I want us to talk about each other and not just about the calendar and the girls. Or the calendar girls.

"Hey, honey! I saw this really great article you'd like on Huffington Post."

"Oh great! I'll read it in the pick-up lane tomorrow, which reminds me that you need to pick up Hadley and get her to the golf course while I take Briley to the dentist."

While softball and various other activities dominate our lives, we have to remember that they are not our entire life. We have to also remember that even though we feel like we are a family divided, we've been brought together through Christ. Like any of his followers, He wants us to be together. Like all of His handiwork, He wants us to live together as one people, one family, one creation.

It's hard—so very hard—but not impossible. The sacrifice of our Messiah, our savior, allows us to be at peace with our situation. Christ's death and resurrection reunites us with not only God our father, but our family here on earth as well.

I take great joy in knowing that one day, our daughters will be (hopefully) productive, independent beings, and Brian and I will get to be together.

I find even greater joy in knowing that the bridge to a relationship with each other and with our Creator has already been built.

Softball takes up a lot of our time and energy. Our Heavenly Father takes up all of our heart.

Our savior and brother, Jesus Christ, You have given us a relationship with our Father and have provided a peace so that we can be brothers and sisters with each other. We're thankful that we can have a full life that comes from You. You are our peace in a very busy and very crowded world. In Your holy name we pray, Amen.

-50-

We Are Family

Then God said, "Let us make humanity in our image to resemble us so that they may take charge of the fish of the sea, the birds in the sky, the livestock, all the earth and all the crawling things are earth." God created humanity in God's own image, in the divine image God created them, male and female, God created them.
Genesis 1:26-27

When I bought my very first computer, I had just graduated from grad school and shortly afterwards, I would meet Brian. The sales guy kept trying to sell me on a dial-up compatible computer. I wasn't sold, but I took my free-month trial disc from AOL and gave it a whirl. That's how new it was.

When Brian and I combined households, we debated on whether or not we'd need the internet. We used a few more free-month discs to help us decide. I'm not sure how it all happened, but it seems like in the blink of an eye, we were all addicted to being online. And by we, I mean, everyone in the world with a phone line and Ethernet cable.

I noticed something with our newly found love for all things world wide web: while we were more connected to anyone we wanted to be connected with (and a few we didn't), we were less connected to the people that we saw face-to-face. I'm 101% certain this is not what God intended when He created us.

Softball and golf and Science Olympiad and youth group—all of these things have allowed us to provide our daughters with actual, real life, face-to-face and not FaceTime relationships. And I'm so grateful.

Last season, the Rebelz played a tournament in Kansas City. As part of the tournament, we got discounted tickets to a Royals game. They were just coming off of a World Series run the season before, and this was just something the team couldn't pass up. The only problem was that the game was on a Thursday night. Many of the parents couldn't get up to Kansas City until Friday evening. So we had to decide—would we keep our girls home and race up Friday evening, missing the Royals game? Or would we send our little player with the parents who could go on Thursday, knowing full-well that they'd take care of them and love them as their own?

When Hadley's last golf season came to an end, we discovered that since most tournaments were during the day, we had very few opportunities to get pictures of our girls on the course. One generous momma spent an afternoon following them as they played a fun round with each other, snapping shots and then doing a team photo shoot after the eighteenth hole. Then she sent us the pictures via email so we could do with them as we pleased.

This is what God intended for our relationships with each other to be. If He wanted us to live in isolation, He'd have created Adam and the Bible would've ended in the middle of Genesis, probably with a very hungry serpent preying upon a very lonely Adam.

We were made to have relationships with others so that we could have a relationship with our Creator. In fact, our Heavenly Father is so intent on being in communion with us that He sent His son Jesus to not only walk among us, having a real-life relationship with us, but to bridge the gap to God for us.

When I send my child away for the weekend with the team or with the youth group, I'm allowing other people to stand in our place ... to be a family to our children.

I'm more grateful than I can express for the family our real-live relationships, especially our softball family, provide for our kiddos and hope that through them, they can see the intentions of God: To do life together and not alone.

You knew, Father, that we could not live this life in isolation. You knew that before Adam was even created. You know now that we often need people to stand as family for us and for our children. And You bless us with amazing people we meet along our life's path. Allow us to be a blessing to others as well. Through our brother Jesus, kind and good, Amen.

-51-

Taking a Break,
or There's More To Life Than Softball

Jesus replied, "The most important one is Israel,
Listen! Our God is the one Lord, and you must love the
Lord your God with all your heart, with all your being,
with all your mind and with all your strength. *The second
is this,* You will love your neighbor as yourself. *No other
commandment is greater than these."*
Mark 12:29-31

As the fall season started winding down, I could see
Briley growing weary. She was practicing with a team
four to five times times a week, going to pitching lessons,
taking hitting lessons, playing school ball and playing
Rebelz ball.

Her exhaustion was tangible, and I was very fearful
that she was about to burn out from her most favorite
thing to do ever at the tender age of eleven and a half.

I was afraid that her dreams of playing softball all
the way through college were about to be shattered
because she had no breathing room from the game.

Slowly, we tapered off the private lessons for just a
little while. School ball ended and with it a lot of her
practice time. She was spending time and weekends

with her Rebelz family and I saw her passion for the game return. It's really amazing what a little breathing room can do for a person.

I cautioned Brian about the off-season. If she wanted to do basketball, which she liked but wasn't passionate about, we'd be fine with it. If she wanted to step up her private lessons or step back from the intensity of them, we'd be fine with it. If she wanted to take on a whole different activity, we would be fine with it because I wanted her to be a well-developed, happy and rested child. Because regardless of her dreams of college ball, she had to first arrive at college with a sound mind and body.

I think she took about ten days of doing nothing before saying she wanted to do something.

She joined Science Olympiad. She began reading her favorite book series again.

She was ecstatic to have more time to be more involved in her youth group, small group and Bible study group, and she asked to start strength and agility training. This would, she told us, help her stay conditioned for softball and would improve her game by improving her strength and speed, two areas she wanted to work on.

The dream was still alive.

I was glad to see her expanding her world a little bit beyond softball. Funny how our daily activities can be so draining when we put our whole being into them.

The exact opposite is true of our relationship with God. The only way to be fully rested and ready for whatever the world throws our way is to devote our whole selves to loving our God and loving each other as we love ourselves.

Whether we are on the softball field or in the gym or at the grocery store, our state of being is greatly improved when our focus is on loving God and each other.

Many times, however, something else takes over center stage in our lives. I often find myself focusing more on social media and marketing my writing and don't always devote the time and energy I should to loving my Lord and God.

Going to church becomes a priority for us as a family in the off-season. It's a great reminder that God needs to be first in our week, and we get to worship with our church family. During the season, we go when we're in town.

When my alarm goes off in the morning, I grab my phone read my devotion (after I hit snooze a few dozen times). I want God to be the great balance in my life. I want all other things in my life to be done to His glory and I want His love to overflow from my activities and behaviors to be shared with others.

I pray that when one activity or another, such as softball, becomes overwhelming to our girls, they will take the time off they need to refocus their time and energies on their Heavenly Father. The rest of their day, their week, their lives will fall into perfect place when we love God first.

165

Father, forgive us when we devote too much time and attention to one part of our lives, neglecting You. Remind us daily through the Spirit's nudging and the interactions with our neighbors that You have created us to love You. That above all else, our full devotion should be directed to You and You alone. Loving You and loving others with that same love is the greatest thing we can do in our lives. It will never make us tired. It will never make us weary. It will always empower and strength us to give more glory to You. In the name of our savior, Jesus Christ, who taught us to love You more dearly, Amen.

-52-

Inside the Circle

Let the heavens rejoice, let the earth be glad;
Let the sea resound, and all that is in it.
Let the field and everything in them be joyful;
let all the trees of the forest sing for joy.
Psalm 96:11-12, New International Version

When my friend, Heather Hawthorne, and I coached our babies during their first season of t-ball. It was so much fun getting to instill a love of the sport in these young baby dolls. Having them follow us around the field like baby ducks follow their mommas was nothing short of comical. Since both of us were married to coaches, we were not only going to teach them to love the game, but to play it properly.

This included them saying, "Yes, coach!" after we gave them their defensive assignment. They were to "hustle" (run as fast as their little legs would carry them) when they were moving from one position to the other whether batting or fielding. They were to say only kind and encouraging words to their teammates as well as the other team's players. And, finally, they were to line up and with a smile, say "Good Game" as we finished that evening's match.

167

As the season began to wind down, we played a game against a team we'd met before. We played our little hearts out for three innings, allowing each girl three at-bats. Then we lined up at home plate ready to "Good Game" our opponents. Almost immediately, I noticed one of our little players, scowling at her opposition and saying, "Not good game" to each of them.

Quickly, I pulled her from the line to see what had been so upsetting to her.

"We lost," she said, crossing her arms across her deflated chest, scowling even more than she had before.

"No we didn't," I consoled her. "We don't even keep score."

She looked at me in a leery way and asked me to confirm this earth-shattering news. "So we didn't lose?"

I shook my head no and she merrily rejoined the line—of the other team—and, with a smile, congratulated her own team with a cherrful "Good game."

The "Good Game" ritual is one of my favorites in the game. I like to see the varsity teams do it; I like to see the college teams do it; I like to see any team, really, meet each other in the center and offer sincere congratulations.

Our current team, however, offers an additional measure to this end-of-game tradition. Once all the "good games" have been offered and high fives have been handed out, our team gathers at the pitcher's mound and prays. They invite the other team—victor or defeated—to join them as well.

Our coaches meet in the circle, and most of the time the other coaches do as well, join hands with their players and bow their heads before God. Usually a player begins the Lord's Prayer and the others join in. When the Amen has been offered, their hands meet in the middle, and it's *softball* on three.

It sounds like a perfect end to any game and that's because it is. To meet in the middle of the place that they all love, the field, and to bow before their Creator who's given them talent and opportunities is just about perfect. Win or lose, they all leave the field joyful—at least for a very small and holy moment.

That's all I ever want for my children … for all children. Long after the days of softball, golf, football, Science Olympiad, Book Club, school, dance, theater, music, whatever … long after those days are gone, I pray that they can stand in their chosen field and find joy in their lives.

Holy and gracious God, who gave us life and all good gifts, thank You mostly for the gift of joy: Joy that comes to us in the form of teammates, family, and even a simple game. You have placed before us a path that should lead to You and have filled that path with perfect gifts. Thank You is not enough for all that You've done for us, so we praise You and worship You with joy in the fields and in every other part of our lives. In the name of Christ our Lord we pray, Amen.

Acknowledgements

I'd like to say that I carefully planned out every single word in this book, but the truth of the matter is that I didn't. The words seemed to come from thin air. We all know that's not true, though. So, for the words that flow effortlessly from me and form coherent sentences, I offer my sincerest and awe-struck thanks to God, my Heavenly Father, who continues to give me good things. It's who He is.

I'm thankful for my daughters, Briley (the softballer) and Hadley (the golfer). They have never known a time that I haven't written about them. They've only run away from home a couple of times a year and reported me to Human Services just a handful of times during the summer. Most of the time, though, they are willing subjects. Great material, girls!

My hubby has stayed up countless hours with me while I was writing. And by stayed up, I mean he slept in the recliner, but it's the thought that counts. I know for a fact I couldn't see my dreams as a writer come true without him. Beyond thankful that I get to do life with him.

My mom was very instrumental in my getting this book written. The times when I needed inspiration, she'd come along and play a Facebook video on her iPad that was so distracting I had no choice but to toss in my earbuds and get a little praise party happening in my head.

Marilyn Boone, Christine Jarmola and Jennifer McMurrain have been reading my words for many years now. Their insight is invaluable, and I couldn't imagine writing a book without their eyes and thoughts. Thank you, friends! I'll cheer for your anatomy anytime. (Also, check out their books—they're great!)

I'm grateful for my editor, Mari Farthing, who signed on to edit with this book as well even though she built a house, moved, and casted a Listen To Your Mother Show during the process. What's that you say? She's a rock star? Couldn't agree with you more.

I'm thrilled to be working with fellow softball mom, Lisa Kuehn of Dream On Marketing, on this project. She designed the cover and made me look all kinds of snazzy. She also packs her own lunches for tournaments. That, my friends, is nothing short of amazing in my world.

I had several good friends who read the first few chapters and told me this was something worth pursuing. A great big thank you and an enthusiastic high five to Stacy Emert, Rachel Hough, Cheryl Holbrook, Cindy Molder and ShaRonda Crow. You mommas make for a great team!

And finally, I'm grateful for you, lovely readers. If it weren't for you, this would just be a lonely little book, sitting on a book shelf. Thanks for reading and praying with me.

About Heather Davis

I am a momma, a writer, a blogger, a humorist, and I have a finely tuned ability to share every last detail of my life with anyone who will read or listen. My first book, TMI Mom Oversharing My Life, is a number 1 best seller, and it has led the way for three more TMI Mom books: Getting Lucky, Crazy on Board and Girlfriend Rules. My fifth book Life With Extra Cheese, was released to rave reviews. When I'm not jetting off to NYC to appear on national talk shows (okay–it's only been one show), I live in Bartlesville with my very patient husband, Brian, and our two crazy daughters. The nuts don't fall far from the tree.

Other Books By Heather Davis

Oversharing My Life
Getting Lucky
Crazy On Board
Girlfriend Rules
Life With Extra Cheese

Available in eBook only

We're Not The Cleavers
Still Not The Cleavers (coming this summer!)
What The Elf Saw

From Life With Extra Cheese

I like to imagine that the ER nurse pulled Dr. Jim Bob to the side and said, "Dude!" as she slapped him upside the head, knocking some sense into him saying they were going to send this incontinent, unable to stand, drawn-faced woman home. The next time he came into the room, he said they were planning on admitting her, and she could see the neurologist on Monday. She'd been in the hospital for over six hours at this point.

I was almost forty-four. My sister was almost forty. But, when I looked at her sitting beside me in that curtain-walled room, I saw a much younger version of my sister.

She was three years old when our dad had his first heart attack. I was seven. Two years later, he had another heart attack and then faced open-heart surgery. I remember sitting at the dinner table one night before we went to Tulsa for the big surgery, and my daddy telling us that he never wanted to be kept alive by machines.

173

In my little kid mind, I imagined that some robot, looking much like R2D2 from Star Wars, continuing to perform CPR on my dad so he wouldn't die.

When my dad had his first stroke almost ten years after his first heart attack, he said the same thing, "I don't want any damn machines keeping me alive."

He also told us that he didn't want us to have a funeral for him because they were too expensive. He wanted to be cremated and then tossed to the side.

At the age of sixteen, I knew my dad's exact plans for his end-of-life. And with each health event that we paced through with my dad, my sister looked exactly the same. She looked like the three year old, tow-headed scared little girl. Regardless of how old she really was.

At the age of sixty-nine, my dad had his final heart attack and final stroke. Having no brain activity at all, we removed him from the life support machines—which looked nothing like R2D2—and three days later, he died. My sister was almost twenty-eight at the time. She looked like she was three.

My mom's plans were very different, though.

They were very different because we never talked about them. I had some ideas, though. I wanted my mom to die when she was ninety-nine years old, peacefully in her sleep in her own home having gone to bed the night before with a sound mind. I wanted her to have her hands crossed on her chest and fresh daisies beside her bed. I wanted the neighborhood birds to be perched above her bedroom window whistling "It Is Well With My Soul."

Sundays At The Field

I wanted my mom to die in a Disney movie, apparently. My way still beats being trampled by wildebeests for sure.

~~~~~~~~~~

As I sat in the emergency room wondering why they didn't just catheterize my mom's bladder already, I realized that all of my plans were changing.

My younger daughter, who had just turned ten, had just joined a competitive softball team. Her schedule was slam-packed with practices, travel and tournaments. My older daughter, who was twelve, was on the middle school golf team and played cello in the orchestra. Not that there's any good time for a stroke to happen, but now was really *not* a good time as far as I was concerned. I didn't ask my mom, but I'm sure she would have agreed.

We didn't have to take my mom to our house that day. She was admitted. I didn't have to go all Macgyver and catheterize her myself with a drinking straw, brightly-patterned duct tape and a Ziploc baggie. I didn't go home that night. I didn't sleep that night.

I did eat a McGaggle's cheeseburger at about nine o'clock that night. My mom looked over at me from her hospital bed and said, "You know that's how this all started."

Made in the USA
Columbia, SC
13 December 2018